HOLLY
SPRINGS

HOLLY SPRINGS

VAN DORN, THE CSS *ARKANSAS* AND THE RAID THAT SAVED VICKSBURG

BRANDON H. BECK

Charleston   London

THE
History
PRESS

Published by The History Press
Charleston, SC 29403
www.historypress.net

First published 2011

Manufactured in the United States

ISBN 978.1.60949.049.2

Library of Congress Cataloging-in-Publication Data
Beck, Brandon H., 1944-
Holly Springs : Van Dorn, the CSS Arkansas, and the raid that saved Vicksburg / Brandon
H. Beck.
p. cm.
Includes bibliographical references.
ISBN 978-1-60949-049-2
1. Holly Springs (Miss.)--History, Military--19th century. 2. Van Dorn, Earl, 1820-1863.
3. Arkansas (Confederate ram) 4. Vicksburg (Miss.)--History--Civil War, 1861-1865. 5.
Mississippi--History--Civil War, 1861-1865--Campaigns. I. Title. II. Title: Van Dorn, the
CSS Arkansas, and the raid that saved Vicksburg.
F349.H79B43 2011
355.009762'88--dc23
2011039232

For Malachi Thomas Beck, born April 3, 2011

Contents

Acknowledgements

I owe many thanks to the following historians, descendants of soldiers, archivists and librarians, guides and photographers. John Anderson, preservation officer of the Texas State Library and Archives Commission, provided me with the photograph of Colonel Griffith. Dr. Mike Ballard, of Mississippi State University, explained some of the fundamental problems of the North Mississippi campaign. Dr. Sid Bondurant, of Grenada, provided information on Van Dorn's route from Streathan's Plantation in Grenada to Houston. Ben Bowen, of Deer Lake, Texas, shared his knowledge of Texas cavalry. Garrie Colhoun, of Holly Springs, is a knowledgeable guide and expert photographer. Susan Chadwell Dignard and Kenneth Hurt agreed to let me use the diary of Lieutenant Alexander Chadwell, 2nd Missouri Cavalry. Joe Douglas, of Columbus, Mississippi, shared his ancestors' experiences in the 1st Mississippi Cavalry. Thanks to John Fox for references to important sources. Gail Gunter, of the Fant Memorial Library of the Mississippi University for Women, was once again a great help with interlibrary loans. Marshall Hudson made the maps; he's painstaking and easy to work with. General Parker Hills shared his insights into Van Dorn's route from Grenada to Holly Springs. Bobby Mitchell, of Holly Springs, shared his knowledge of Hill Crest Cemetery. I'm grateful to

Darren Moran for bringing Captain Robert J. Kyle's article in *Army History* to my attention. Tom Parrish, author of *The Saga of the Confederate Ram "Arkansas"* (1987), gave me encouragement, insight and pictures from that great book. Don Paul brought the Fletcher Pomeroy diary to my attention and sent me a copy. Eric Politzer directed me to the newsletter of the Congressional Cemetery for his article about Colonel Murphy. The staff of the Harriette Person Memorial Library in Port Gibson kindly sent me information about the Confederate monument in Port Gibson, which bears Van Dorn's likeness. Bob Price is an expert on Confederate monuments and an expert photographer. Jim Reeves, of Columbus, Mississippi, opened his library to me. Thanks to John Rice III, of Oxford, for bringing the *Northeast Mississippi Daily Journal*'s article "At the Crossroads: Northeast Mississippi in the Civil War" to my attention. Jessie Riggs, of Caledonia, Mississippi, brought important sources to my attention also. Bob Schmidt, of French Village, Missouri, author of *"Boys of the Best Families in the State": Co. E, 2nd Missouri Confederate Cavalry*, introduced me to Lieutenant Alexander Chadwell and helped secure Susan Dignard's permission to quote from his diary. Lois Swaney Shipp, of the Marshall County Historical Museum in Holly Springs, introduced me to Holly Springs. Terrence Winschell, park historian at the Vicksburg National Battlefield Park, was a very great help, as was Anne Webster at the Mississippi Department of Archives and History. Time and again, staffers at both Vicksburg and MDAH answered questions that arose in research.

The Holly Springs Tourism Bureau and the Blue and Gray Education Society placed a series of informative historical markers in Holly Springs. They make up an informative self-guided tour. General Parker Hills was their chief consultant.

In Holly Springs, Garrie Colhoun and Jim Thomas gave me many hours of their time helping me understand the geographical setting of the country between Grenada and Holly Springs and of Holly Springs itself. I could not have had two better historian-guides.

My wife, Melissa, typed the manuscript and improved the narrative. My grateful thanks to her.

Introduction

On July 4, 1863, Union troops raised the flag of the United States over Vicksburg, Mississippi. Situated on bluffs high over the Mississippi River, about midway between Memphis, Tennessee, and New Orleans, Louisiana, Vicksburg had enormous strategic and symbolic importance. To President Lincoln, it was the "key" to the unvexed flow of the river from the upper Midwest to the Gulf of Mexico. To President Jefferson Davis, it was the "nail-head" that held the Confederate Trans-Mississippi—Louisiana, Arkansas and Texas—to the eastern states.

Two previous attempts to take Vicksburg had failed. In the summer of 1862, the Union threat came from the Mississippi River, as ships of the United States Navy came up from New Orleans and down from Memphis in an effort to compel the city to surrender. In the fall of 1862, the threat came from Grant's Army of the Tennessee, moving down the line of the Mississippi Central Railroad through the heart of North Mississippi. Both campaigns were turned back.

The Confederate officer most responsible for the successful defense of Vicksburg was the colorful and controversial Major General Earl Van Dorn (1827–1863). Van Dorn is known more for his defeats at Elkhorn Tavern and Corinth than for his defense of Vicksburg. But the story of Van Dorn and Vicksburg involves two of the most dramatic moments in

Civil War history—the voyage of the CSS *Arkansas* and the raid on Holly Springs. Van Dorn bought Vicksburg time, putting off its fall for over a year. Van Dorn was assassinated at his headquarters in Spring Hill, Tennessee, on May 7, 1863, and did not live to see Vicksburg surrender.

Chapter 1

Vicksburg

*"Mississippians Don't Know, and Refuse to Learn,
How to Surrender"*

Along its length of 2,320 miles, the Mississippi River borders ten states, gives its name to one and connects them all with New Orleans, already the world's fourth-largest port twenty years before the Civil War. The river brought Vicksburg into being, on the east bank, first as Walnut Hills in 1814. It was incorporated in 1825 and soon bore the name Vicksburg, named for Newitt Vick, a planter and Methodist preacher, who died in 1819. His descendants named the town for him. Roughly equidistant between New Orleans and Memphis, Vicksburg's great attraction for settlers was the agricultural potential of land drained by both the Mississippi and the Yazoo River, which empties into the Mississippi just upstream. In the 1830s, the railroads came to complement the rivers. By the time of the Civil War, the Southern Railroad of Mississippi connected Vicksburg with Jackson, fifty miles east, and with Meridian, on the Mobile & Ohio Railroad in southeast Mississippi. The New Orleans, Jackson & Great Northern Railroad connected Vicksburg, via Grenada and the Mississippi Central Railroad, to Grand Junction, Tennessee, and the Memphis & Charleston Railroad in northeast Mississippi. That line crossed the Mobile & Ohio Railroad at Corinth. A third line served Vicksburg from Louisiana—the Vicksburg, Shreveport & Texas Railroad—which had its eastern

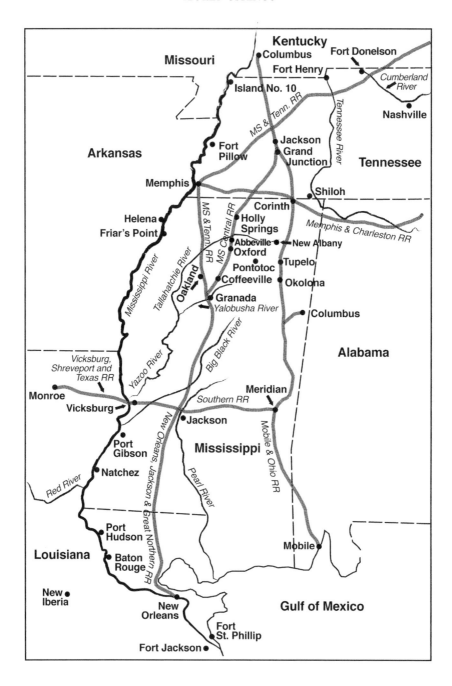

Vicksburg Campaigns, 1862. General Area. *By Marshall Hudson.*

terminus on De Soto Point, the peninsula formed by the river's hairpin turn across from Vicksburg.[1]

Vicksburg was the county seat of Warren County. Vicksburg's population in 1860 was about 5,000, including about 1,400 slaves. From the cupola of the fine courthouse, finished in 1860, one could see out over the river to the Louisiana shore. "Riverboat traffic clogged the landing. More long staple cotton was shipped from Vicksburg than from any other city in the world."[2] King Cotton ruled. As the decade of the 1850s drew to a close in the impending national crisis, Vicksburg and Warren County stood together. Slavery was an integral part of the economy and culture. Abolition was unthinkable. But secession—let alone war— was almost equally so. Mississippi was the first state to follow South Carolina out of the Union, joining it on January 9, 1861. But in elections to the Secession Convention, Vicksburg chose Unionist delegates by 561 to 175.[3] There was no question, however, that town and county would stay with their state, hoping that war would not come to them. But as Michael Ballard has written, "The very thing that gave economic life to the town, the Mississippi, would likewise bring destruction…the United States, not the Southern states, had controlled the Mississippi for nearly sixty years."[4] It was unrealistic, if understandable, to hope that the Northern states would believe that the Confederate states would leave the river open for commerce bound for New Orleans. Louisiana's governor, Thomas Moore, and Mississippi's John Pettus both feared Union efforts to force the issue, either by landing troops or shelling towns along the river. On January 11, overzealous state troops at Vicksburg fired at an unarmed and innocent steamer coming upriver.[5]

A month later, Mississippi's Jefferson Davis became provisional president of the Confederate States of America. The news came to him at his plantation, Briarfield, some forty miles south of Vicksburg. On February 11, he came upriver to Vicksburg for the train to Jackson and made his first speech as Confederate president. He described his long struggle to maintain constitutional equality among the states. He went on: "Our safety and honor required us to dissolve our connection with the United States. I hope that our separation may be peaceful. But whether it be so or not, I am ready, as I always have been, to redeem my pledges to you and the South by shedding every drop of my blood in your cause."[6] Neither he, Mississippi nor Vicksburg could turn back now.

A year passed before Davis's formal inauguration in Richmond in February 1862. By that time, Confederate military fortunes had begun to sink, particularly in the west, the vast area between the Appalachians and the Mississippi River.[7]

In February 1862, Brigadier General Ulysses S. Grant and Navy Flag Officer Andrew Hull Foote dealt the Confederacy a deadly blow, capturing Fort Henry on February 6 and Fort Donelson on February 16, located at the mouths of the Tennessee and Cumberland Rivers, respectively. The victories opened both rivers for hundreds of miles upstream to the gunboats and troop transports of the U.S. Navy.

The loss of the forts unhinged the Confederate defense of Kentucky and Middle Tennessee. Confederate General Albert Sydney Johnston ordered the evacuations of Bowling Green and Nashville, the first state capital to fall to the Union. Johnston was able to concentrate his army at Corinth, where General P.G.T. Beauregard joined him as his second in command. Charles P. Roland, the biographer of Albert Sidney Johnston, has described Corinth as the most important town in the western Confederacy, the point where the Memphis & Charleston and Mobile & Ohio Railroads crossed. Today, the city of Corinth describes that crossing as "the most important sixteen feet of land in the Confederacy." Johnston's narrow but costly defeat at Shiloh, on April 5–6, just north of Corinth on the Tennessee River, cost him his life and put Corinth in danger.

If Corinth fell, the Confederates would lose both the rail junction and the eastern approach to Memphis, including the connection at Grand Junction with the Mississippi Central Railroad to Holly Springs and Grenada. General Beauregard, who succeeded Johnston in command after Johnston's death at Shiloh, believed that the loss of Corinth would endanger the entire Mississippi Valley.[8]

Beauregard prepared to defend Corinth against Grant's successor, General Henry W. Halleck. As Halleck moved slowly toward Corinth, another great disaster befell the Confederacy. Between April 25 and May 1, the U.S. Navy's West Gulf Blockading Squadron, under the command of Flag Officer David Farragut, took New Orleans. Before the Union

Henry W. Halleck, 1815–1872. Halleck occupied Corinth, Mississippi, on May 30, 1862, and then became general in chief of all U.S. armies in July, a post he held until 1864. *From* The Photographic History of the Civil War in Ten Volumes, *ed. Francis Trevelyan Miller, vol. 10.*

David Glasgow Farragut, 1801–1870. His West Gulf Blockading Squadron took New Orleans, Baton Rouge and Natchez, but not Vicksburg. *From* The Photographic History of the Civil War in Ten Volumes, *ed. Francis Trevelyan Miller, vol. 1.*

army moved in, Confederate General Mansfield Lovell moved his men and artillery to safety in Jackson. The Southern Railroad of Mississippi then brought them to Vicksburg.[9] But in taking the largest city in the Confederacy, Farragut had gained an invaluable blockading station for his squadron. He had also opened the mouth of the Mississippi to Union warships, just as taking Fort Henry and Fort Donelson had opened the Tennessee and the Cumberland Rivers to the Union. The possibility of seizing control of the Mississippi's entire length now loomed large. President Lincoln had seen it the previous November, telling Admiral David D. Porter then that the river could not be completely controlled until Vicksburg was in their hands.[10]

Why, exactly, was Vicksburg so important? Its significance was twofold. First, it was the strongest (thought to be impassable) barrier to river traffic, from the upper Midwest to the Gulf. Second, it was the essential link in a logistical (supply) chain, crossing the river from the Trans-Mississippi to the Confederate states east of the river. After the fall

"This focus of Secession, Vicksburg, with its high bluffs, crowned with batteries."—Union General Thomas R. Williams. *From* The Photographic History of the Civil War in Ten Volumes, *ed. Francis Trevelyan Miller, vol. 1.*

of New Orleans, the only Confederate towns on the river with railroad connections to the east were Memphis and Vicksburg. Vicksburg, built on bluffs high over the river, overlooked a hairpin turn in the river below, a turn of about 180 degrees in a half mile, a virtual U-turn that actually turned the river north before it came south again.[11] The great bend is no longer there; the river changed its course in 1878, but in 1862, it was in full view from artillery positions overlooking the river. Confederate artillery had a field of fire over three miles of the river's length, exactly at the point where anything moving upstream would be further slowed and exposed in the sharp bend.[12]

The great bend enhanced Vicksburg's importance as a logistical cross-river link. It created the peninsula known as De Soto Point, the terminus of the Vicksburg, Shreveport & Texas Railroad. Confederate ferries and river skiffs could carry both men and supplies across the river under the protection of the same guns that blocked traffic headed down the river. "Railroads and riverboats made it the principal transfer point across the Mississippi River south of Memphis. Supplies of all kinds, following a path from as far away as Matamoros in Mexico, crossed the river at Vicksburg."[13] Most important of these supplies were vast quantities of sugar, molasses and salt, important for consumption but also as "commodity money" for the purchase of beef in the eastern Confederacy.[14]

Seen in this way, the old description of Vicksburg as "Confederate Gibraltar" takes on more meaning. But after the fall of New Orleans, Vicksburg seemed very un-Gibraltar-like—it seemed vulnerable. Farragut came quickly upstream, taking Baton Rouge, 160 miles south of Vicksburg, on May 9 and Natchez, 75 miles south, on May 12. On May 18, the lead ships of his squadron—five warships and two troop transports—commanded by Captain S. Phillips Lee, reached Vicksburg.

From atop the bluffs, some twenty stories high, the Federal ships seemed small, even tiny, as they steamed slowly toward the town, but they were larger than anything Vicksburgians had seen this far upriver, slender and graceful with tall sailing masts that seemed completely out of place on the Mississippi, as did the great black 11-inch cannons that lined their gun decks.[15]

Captain Lee and his officers could see only two batteries, of no more than four guns each. They probably expected a repetition of the surrender formalities at Baton Rouge and Natchez. At 12:20 p.m., Captain Lee ordered a gig, a light ship's boat, from the *Oneida* to be manned and lowered. He gave its officer a message for the "Authorities at Vicksburg"—a demand for their immediate surrender. The gig ran up a white flag and started toward the landing. "Suddenly, one of the guns on the hill roared into action. A single projectile came whistling across the bow of the boat flying the flag of truce. This was the first shot fired by the Vicksburg defenders against their foe. The gig stopped. A steamer put out from the wharf to see what the Federals wanted."[16] When the steamer reached the gig, a Federal officer handed over the note; he would return at 3:00 p.m. for the reply—a mere formality, it would seem.

Vicksburg was in General Mansfield Lovell's department. Although he had not been able to defend New Orleans, he had worked hard to prepare the defense of Vicksburg.[17] Lovell had named Brigadier General Martin Luther Smith, a skilled engineer, to command the post. Smith had only about three thousand men in his garrison, but work on the batteries was going ahead rapidly. Within the next two days, eighteen heavy guns were installed, more of them near the water's edge than on the bluffs.[18] There was no thought of surrender. Lee's demand brought three replies: from Mayor Lazarus Lindsay, General Smith and Lieutenant Colonel J.L. Autry, military governor and post commander for the state. All were adamant refusals. Smith refused to surrender on his honor as a soldier. Mayor Lindsay replied that "neither the municipal authorities nor the citizens will consent to a surrender of the city."[19] Autry's was the most defiant: "I have to state that Mississippians don't know, and refuse to learn, how to surrender to an enemy."[20]

There was little the Federals could do to compel Vicksburg to surrender, even after the rest of Farragut's ships arrived. Farragut soon took his oceangoing vessels back to New Orleans, leaving only six gunboats behind to blockade the river and carry on an intermittent and largely ineffective bombardment. He would not return until mid-June.

After the loss of Nashville, Baton Rouge and New Orleans, President Davis welcomed Vicksburg's defiance. But bad news continued to come in from everywhere else. General Beauregard evacuated Corinth on May 30, falling back to Tupelo. What Union General Halleck would do next with the huge force at his disposal—the Army of the Ohio, the Army of the Mississippi and Grant's Army of the Tennessee—remained to be seen. But on June 6, Memphis fell to Flag Officer Charles Davis's Western Gunboat Flotilla and a ram squadron led by Colonel Charles Ellet Jr. Vicksburg was now the only Confederate post on the Mississippi with railroad connections to the east, and it was vulnerable from both upstream and downstream.

In Richmond, President Davis was determined to hold Vicksburg and reverse the incoming tide of disasters. He shared Autry's spirit of defiance; Autry's words could easily have been his. He knew that General Smith was an excellent and hardworking engineer. But since the fall of New Orleans, he had lost confidence in Smith's superior, department commander General Lovell. On June 14, he wrote Smith, asking: "What

Martin Luther Smith, 1819–
1866. A New Yorker who served
the South first as major of
engineers and later as major
general. He earned the trust of
Van Dorn and later Robert E.
Lee. *From* The Photographic
History of the Civil War in Ten
Volumes, *ed. Francis Trevelyan
Miller, vol. 10.*

is the condition of your defenses at Vicksburg? Can we do anything to aid you? Disasters above and below increase the value of your position."[21] Smith replied that he was confident in the strength of his batteries but he needed more infantry. The great need, however, was for a "clear-headed general officer."[22]

Davis agreed and went into action to find one. His first choice was Major General John B. Magruder. Magruder had done well in the early stages of the Peninsula Campaign, east of Richmond, but had disappointed General Robert E. Lee in the following Seven Days' Campaign. For unspecified reasons, Magruder would be significantly delayed in arriving in Mississippi. "The necessity is urgent and absolute," Davis wrote to his second choice, Major General Braxton Bragg, then commanding a corps under Beauregard at Tupelo. Davis, however, had as little confidence in Beauregard as he did in Lovell, and so when Beauregard, tired and ill after Shiloh and Corinth, insisted that he needed Bragg at Tupelo "as I am leaving for a while…I must have a short rest,"[23] Davis reacted quickly. On June 17, he replaced Beauregard—with Bragg. He then continued his search for a replacement for Lovell. On June 19, he chose Major General Earl Van Dorn, then commanding the Army of the West near Tupelo, ordering him to "assume command of the Department of South Mississippi and East Louisiana."[24]

President Davis explained to Mississippi's Governor Pettus, "My efforts to provide for the military wants of your section have been sadly frustrated…Last evening [Beauregard's departure] became known to me, and I sent a telegram directing General Van Dorn…to assume the command of the Department of Southern Mississippi and East Louisiana. I hope he will answer the popular desire."[25]

Davis's appointment had brought Van Dorn home to the Mississippi River. Van Dorn was born in 1820 in Port Hudson, about thirty miles south of Vicksburg. He was the great-nephew of President Andrew Jackson, whose influence secured him an appointment at West Point, in the class of 1842. He finished fifty-second of fifty-six in the class.[26] He had been a soldier all his life, and he was frequently separated from his wife Caroline Godbold, whom he married in Alabama in 1845.[27] He had a distinguished record in the Mexican War, in the 7th Infantry, and was wounded at least once. Jefferson Davis noted that Van Dorn "had been quite as often noticed in official reports for gallantry and good conduct as any officer who served in that war."[28]

After the Mexico War, Van Dorn served with great distinction in Texas with the famous 2nd Cavalry Regiment, initially under the command of Robert E. Lee. He attracted the attention of Major General David Twiggs, who placed him in command of two successful expeditions against the Comanche Indians. He was wounded several times, twice seriously, on October 1, 1858. One arrow skewered his forearm, and another passed through his ribcage from right to left. He extracted both arrows himself.[29]

He was, without doubt, bold and courageous. One observer described Van Dorn in 1861: "The general is of a spare frame, erect and graceful… his mustache is long but bright; otherwise he is cleanly shaven…his uniform was a gray tunic, with buff collar and cuffs, heavy gild braiding

Earl Van Dorn,
1820–1863. An early
wartime photograph.
*Courtesy of Mississippi
Department of Archives
and History (MDAH).*

on the sleeves and three stars on each side of his collar...as he drew back on his buck gauntlets, I caught sight of a cross...embroidered there in scarlet silk."[30] A more modern southern historian described him as having "one of those antebellum faces full of tumult and recklessness, which truly exposed his spirit."[31]

In 1861, Van Dorn resigned his commission six days before Mississippi seceded. He served first as brigadier general of State Troops, second in command to Jefferson Davis. Davis later wrote that Van Dorn "was associated with me in the organization of this army in Mississippi, immediately after the secession of our state and I was sincerely attached to him."[32]

Van Dorn admired the president but chafed under the yoke of administrative duties. He was glad to be sent to Texas. There, he recruited men and coordinated the transfer or seizure of Federal forts and smaller posts to Confederate authority. On April 17, in a bold operation carried out with Texas militia units, he captured the USS *Star of the West* at Matagordo Bay. There were some complaints about the faulty logistical arrangements he had made for the Texas troops moving across Louisiana and then over the Mississippi.[33] But rapid promotions followed: to brigadier general on June 5 and to major general on September 14. He served briefly in Virginia until January 1862.[34] He then came back west as a district commander in the Trans-Mississippi Department. Van Dorn thought in large terms, however, looking for an opportunity for his Army of the West, seventeen thousand strong, to advance into Missouri and take St. Louis. But the result was a stinging defeat—nearly two thousand casualties at the Battle of Elkhorn Tavern (Pea Ridge, Arkansas) on March 2, 1862. Trying to put the best face on it, he maintained that "I was not defeated, but only failed in my intentions."[35]

On March 17, Van Dorn took his force across the Mississippi, hoping to join General Johnston's army as it reconcentrated at Corinth. The combination of distance, miserable weather and the condition of the roads prevented him from reaching Johnston in time for the Battle of Shiloh (April 5–6). When his force did arrive, late in April, he moved into Beauregard's defenses around Corinth. At the end of May, he concurred with Beauregard's other subordinates—Generals Leonidas Polk, Braxton Bragg and John C. Breckinridge—that there was no alternative to evacuation.[36] He remained in command of the Army of the West until he was summoned to Vicksburg.

His career so far had been fast moving and oft changing, with mixed results. He had great self-confidence, even though his surviving correspondence reveals that he was frustrated and yearned for greatness.[37]

Vicksburg received him enthusiastically with serenades and other pleasantries. Van Dorn reported to the president on June 22: "I arrived here yesterday. I find large fleets of gun-boats, mortar-boats, and transports, with troops arriving and descending the river toward Vicksburg…Will defend to the death." He added later, "Will not give up unless beaten back by superior force. Foot by foot the city will be sacrificed. Of course, citizens proud to do so."[38] In the words of Mississippi's Governor Pettus, Van Dorn stood ready "to flash defiance in the face of the enemies of Mississippi."[39] In August, the South Carolinian poet Paul Hamilton Hayne wrote a poetic salute to the defenders of Vicksburg entitled "Vicksburg: A Ballad." He dedicated it to Van Dorn, "our bold young leader."

Chapter 2

"Our Bold Young Leader" and the CSS *Arkansas*

On June 18, Admiral Farragut returned to Vicksburg. He saw that the defenses were far stronger than when he had sailed away. His own force was also stronger. It now included General Thomas William's infantry force of three thousand men. Also, Captain David D. Porter's Mortar Flotilla, the "bombers," and their accompanying steamers had left New Orleans on June 13–14 and were at Vicksburg by June 19–20. The mortars significantly increased the fleet's firepower. These stub-barreled guns made up for their short range and low velocity with an extremely high arc of fire—their shells fell vertically, down on targets as high as some of the Vicksburg batteries. Mortar fire could destroy the guns or drive the crews to shelters while ships passed the batteries. Soon, Flag Officer Charles M. Davis's Western Gunboat Flotilla would bring even more mortars, along with ironclads, rams and timberclads downriver from Memphis. Army Lieutenant Colonel Alfred Ellet's Ram Squadron was at the mouth of the Yazoo, six miles upstream from Vicksburg, by June 24.[40]

Van Dorn knew that he needed help on the river, but the Confederacy had no Mississippi flotilla comparable to Farragut's armada. The Confederate River Defense Fleet had been wiped out at New Orleans and Memphis. Two unfinished ironclads, the *Louisiana* and the *Mississippi*, had been lost at New Orleans, and the *Tennessee*, also unfinished, had been lost at Memphis.[41] A few smaller vessels—cottonclads and the ironclad ram *Van Dorn*—were taken down from Memphis to the Yazoo and then up to Greenwood, Mississippi, just in time to escape Davis.

Also escaping, but not under its own power, was the unfinished CSS *Arkansas*. It was intended as an ironclad, 180 feet long. Just before the fall of Memphis, the wooden hull was towed downstream and then up the Yazoo to Greenwood. A barge carrying what armor the Memphis builders had on hand followed behind. The ship was far from ready and, under the circumstances, might never have been finished. Her "biographer," Thomas Parrish, describes her as a symbol of "the South's unfaltering resolution to wage war despite her industrial destitution and technological deficiencies."[42] Another writer described her as "a rusty hulk…no deckhouse and no engines…a floating wreck."[43] Even worse, the barge carrying the iron sank in the Yazoo.

The obstacles to transforming the hull into a warship seemed insurmountable, but after May 28, she had a chance: the navy put the right man in charge of finishing her—Naval Lieutenant Isaac Newton Brown, the former commander of the naval yard at New Orleans. Brown's orders were to finish the ship, "without regard to expenditure of men or money." He went to work immediately. "Taking a day to fish up the sunken iron," he then towed his project downstream to Yazoo City, where she arrived on June 4. Yazoo City was a river port with some steamboat facilities. He placed obstructions downstream to protect the ship as the work went on and brought in more railroad iron by wagon from the nearest railroad depot, most likely at Vaughn. Among Van Dorn's first decisions at Vicksburg was to ask President Davis to place the ship under his orders. Davis immediately assented.[44]

Lieutenant Brown brought energy and ingenuity to the task, putting two hundred men to work day and night. He had fourteen iron forges in constant operation. Brown pushed his crews hard, even jailing workmen who "were inclined to trifle with him."[45]

But the ship remained a mystery and was far from unveiling. General M.L. Smith thought on June 15 that she was close to ready,[46] but the work could not be completed before mid-July. Army officers eagerly

Isaac Newton Brown, 1817–1889. Builder and commander of the CSS *Arkansas*. On July 15, 1862, his ship fought "without the fear of hitting a friend or missing an enemy." *From* The Saga of the Confederate Ram "Arkansas": The Mississippi Valley Campaign *by Tom Z. Parrish, 1987.*

anticipated her coming down but may not have fully understood the problems Brown would face sailing his ship, if and when he completed her.[47] Brown's problems were immense. The ship's weight could prove too much for the engines he had on hand, and her speed and mobility would suffer as a result. Most Confederate ironclads were capable only of "a slow four knots," i.e., 4.6 miles per hour. She would also ride low in the water, an additional problem in the summer months on the Yazoo and the Mississippi, when water levels fell. Brown worried about Union ships coming through his raft at the mouth of the Yazoo, but his biggest problem, he wrote on June 22, was in getting a crew. He was going to need help from Smith in Vicksburg to fill his complement. "My attention is entirely required in getting the *Arkansas* ready…I will do what I can to injure the enemy."[48]

Union apprehension ran as high as Confederate anticipation. Ellet, whose rams were now at the mouth of the Yazoo, had heard rumors of a powerful ship of some kind being built upstream. He sent two rams upriver to investigate.[49] Near the mouth of the tributary Big Sunflower, they came in sight of the Confederate cottonclads and the *Van Dorn*. The Confederate commander panicked and ordered his crews to scuttle his three ships. According to the log of the Union ram *Lancaster*, "When the Van Dorn blew up [it] shook the hills. Finding we could not get by, we rounded to and started back. We had a good view of the *Arkansas* lying above the raft."[50] The lightly armed rams then returned to the Mississippi. Van Dorn, enraged by the loss of the ships, demanded that the officer responsible be brought before a court-martial.[51] But the *Arkansas* was safe, still veiled in mystery.

Davis's and Farragut's ships were now six river miles apart, separated by the great bend in the river. They communicated with each other by land.[52] Farragut and Davis faced the question of whether the navy alone could compel Vicksburg to surrender. The infantry force on hand, Williams's Brigade, was too small to risk in a landing. There seemed to be no help coming from Halleck's huge force, now divided for purposes Halleck deemed more important than taking Vicksburg, i.e., taking Chattanooga. The navy was on its own at Vicksburg.

Farragut believed that if he had any chance of battering Vicksburg into submission, it would be by bringing his mortars and heaviest guns directly to bear on the batteries, destroying Vicksburg's defenses in an "organized steaming" to join Davis's fleet upriver. If they could run the batteries under the plunging fire of the mortars and direct fire from the big naval guns while pushing upriver, the combined fleets might be able to do it again with even better results coming downriver.[53]

Between June 20 and June 27, the bombardment was very heavy, reaching a peak on the evening of the twenty-seventh. Farragut's run upriver began early on the morning of the twenty-eighth. Smith estimated that "some thirty-five vessels were soon firing as rapidly as was possible, the mortars filling the air with shells, and the sloops of war and gunboats delivering broadside after broadside...continuing and deafening."[54] Van Dorn described the bombardment as "heavy yesterday and this morning...No flinching...all sound and fury, and to brave men contemptible."[55]

But Farragut succeeded, passing through the fire of twenty-six cannon trained on the river, in an ordeal lasting two hours, returning fire, pushing hard to round the great bend.[56] It was an important moment: passing the batteries showed that Confederate Vicksburg no longer had undisputed control of even the length of the river within reach of its guns.[57] However, it brought the navy's siege no closer to success. Within an hour of rounding the bend, Farragut wrote, "I passed up the river this morning, but to no purpose...It is not possible for us to take Vicksburg without an army force of twelve to fifteen thousand men."[58]

The infantry force that had come upriver with Farragut, General Thomas Williams's small division, was, for want of any better use, put to work with impressed slaves, digging a canal across the base of De Soto Point. A successful canal, one and a half miles long, would turn the point into an island. The new channel would bypass the Vicksburg batteries. At the very least, Williams's men could, and did, destroy the western terminus of the Vicksburg, Shreveport & Texas Railroad.[59]

There was nothing Van Dorn could do to defeat the canal project. He did work tirelessly to bolster his command's strength, bringing in heavy guns from Mobile and Columbus, Mississippi, and adding troops from wherever he could find them, citing orders from General Bragg. Bragg himself sent him General John C. Breckinridge's division, which reached Vicksburg on June 28, bringing the garrison up to about fifteen thousand

John C. Breckinridge, 1821–1875. Former vice president of the United States, he served Van Dorn well at Vicksburg, Baton Rouge and Port Hudson. *From* The Photographic History of the Civil War in Ten Volumes, *ed. Francis Trevelyan Miller, vol. 10.*

men.[60] Van Dorn and Breckinridge got along well at first, once manning a gun together and exchanging fire with a gunboat. Relations became more formal as time passed, however.

Van Dorn issued his Special Orders No. 5 on June 28. The orders began with a firm declaration—"General Van Dorn assumes command in person of the defense of Vicksburg and surrounding country"—and ended with a stirring call for duty and sacrifice: "Let it be borne in mind that the army here is defending the place against occupation. This will be done at all hazards, even though this beautiful and devoted city should be laid in ruins and ashes."

"The people will sustain you in your heroic endeavor," President Davis assured him. General Smith concurred, but Van Dorn seemed not so certain. In what he later described as a "broad, catholic spirit, wide as our country," Van Dorn meant to put public officials—even civil law—under military authority.[61] He incurred the wrath of Louisiana's governor, Thomas Moore, by seizing rifles and ammunition from supply depots in his state. "I demand the return of 2,720 rifles and ammunition seized by General Van Dorn," Moore wrote to the War Department in Richmond.[62] Secretary of War George Randolph, with help from the president, managed to placate the governor.[63]

But Van Dorn went even further. On July 4, exactly a year before Vicksburg surrendered, Van Dorn issued his General Orders No. 9, putting eleven counties in Mississippi and "all the counties in Louisiana east of the Mississippi River" under martial law, defined as "the will of the military commander." "Disloyalty must and will not be countenanced. The credit of the Government must be sustained. The seeds of dissention and dissatisfaction shall not be sown among the troops. Speculation and extortion upon soldiers and citizens will not be tolerated." Punishments included fines, imprisonment, impressments, censorship—including denial of the right to publish—and confiscation. Those attempting to trade with or give information to the enemy, or pass into enemy lines "without a passport from the proper authority, shall suffer death."[64]

The proclamation unleashed a storm of protest against Van Dorn, one that raged from Vicksburg to Richmond. Van Dorn may have exaggerated the willingness (or unwillingness) of civilians to sacrifice everything or the extent of the offenses he singled out in the proclamation. But he certainly understood the gravity of the military situation. Van Dorn has had many critics, and of more than one aspect of his life, but no one questions his devotion to the cause of Southern independence. He and General Smith believed that the Federal bombardment of Vicksburg violated the rules of civilized warfare and justified an extraordinary response.[65] It should be noted that Terrence Winschell, park historian at Vicksburg National Battlefield Park, has stated that "Federal guns were not directed against the city and its population" but instead at the batteries, many of which were near residential and commercial areas. During the naval siege, incoming fire was from maximum range with minimal accuracy. There was damage to private property, but fortunately, only two residents were killed.

Meanwhile, Lieutenant Brown was making amazing progress with his ship at Yazoo City. Lieutenant George Gift marveled at Brown's labors: "Within five weeks from the day we arrived at Yazoo City we had a man-of-war (such as she was) from almost nothing."[66] By mid-July, the hulk towed down from Memphis in early June had become a twin screw propeller vessel, clad with railroad iron, 165 feet long, 35 feet at the beam, with a draft of 11½ feet. Brown wrote, "The *Arkansas* now appeared as if a small sea-going vessel had been cut down to the water's edge at both ends, leaving a box for guns amidships." The straight sides of the box were 1-foot-thick oak within a layer of iron. The ends were closed in by timber 1 foot square, planked over with six-inch strips of oak, the whole then encased in a shell of iron set at an angle of thirty-five degrees in order to deflect shot. The sides were pierced with apertures for ten guns. Although one of Brown's most vexing problems had been in building her gun carriages, his ship was heavily armed, mounting ten guns in all: two eight-inch 64-pounders at the bow, two rifled 32-pounders astern and two 100-pounder Columbiads and a six-inch naval gun on each side.[67] He had thirteen excellent officers and a crew of two hundred—"seamen, landsmen, firemen, soldiers and boys," including about fifty Missouri infantrymen—under Captain Samuel Harris.[68] Brown was sure of his crew, although many lacked any experience remotely resembling what they were in for now. "The only trouble they gave me," Brown wrote,

The *Arkansas* at Yazoo City. Brown's drilling machines were on the deck of the steamer *Capitol* (right). Crews worked night and day drilling bolt holes in railroad iron to fasten onto the *Arkansas*. *From* The Saga of the Confederate Ram "Arkansas": The Mississippi Valley Campaign *by Tom Z. Parrish, 1987.*

"was to keep them from running the *Arkansas* into the Union fleet before we were ready for battle."[69]

The *Arkansas* had the potential to change the balance of naval power on the Mississippi. Winston Groom has commented that "except for her engines…the *Arkansas* was a match for any Federal ironclad on station above Vicksburg. Whether she would prove a match for all of them and Farragut's big men-of-war and gunboats, remained to be seen.[70] Her weakness lay in the worst place—her engines: two low-pressure engines, producing nine hundred horsepower. They had great potential for power and speed. Brown estimated that they could make eight miles per hour in still water. But they were unpredictable and prone to breaking down. They operated independently of each other, propelling and maneuvering the ship. If one broke down, the other could overpower the rudder, with dire consequences. Lieutenant George Gift spotted another weakness: the boilers were not lined on the facing side with non-conducting material, which meant "the whole mass of iron about the boilers became red hot."[71]

Brown may have thought that the combination of suspect engines and the summer's falling water levels in the Yazoo and Mississippi made the ship better able to defend the Yazoo than to go down into the Mississippi. But his account shows that while he was anxious to move while he still could, he simply needed more time to ready the ship for battle. Van Dorn may have misinterpreted Brown's caution as reluctance to come down at all.[72]

Brown's accomplishment at Yazoo City was little short of miraculous; the *Arkansas* would not have existed without him. But as Thomas Parrish has written, "If credit for the *Arkansas*' conception belongs to [Secretary of the Navy Stephen] Mallory, and if Lt. Brown's élan pushed the ram to completion, it was General Earl Van Dorn who first felt the urge to fling the cotton field monster in the enemy's face."[73] Sensing Brown's caution, he began to exert pressure. The message he sent Brown, through General Daniel Ruggles on June 24, reads like a challenge: "Can you send messenger to the commander of the ram *Arkansas* and suggest to him [Brown] to come out, run the fleet, and get behind them and sink transports? If he is fast enough he can do this easily. He could clear the river below. It is better to die game and do some execution than to lie by and be burned up in the Yazoo."[74]

Van Dorn wrote to Brown directly on July 12, telling him he would face as many as thirty-seven ships in combined fleets at Vicksburg.[75] "She has much to contend with here," Van Dorn wrote to the president on July 14, but "better to let her try her strength than to get aground in the Yazoo and be burnt up like the rest."[76]

Brown was as brave as he was capable. He was under Van Dorn's orders, but he was a sailor and Van Dorn was not. Understandably reluctant to sacrifice his ship in a hopeless mission, Brown sent Lieutenant Charles Read to Vicksburg to speak with Van Dorn, probably on July 11. Read rode all night to reach Vicksburg early in the morning. He met Van Dorn, finding him courteous but unyielding. Read wrote that "the general thoroughly appreciated the importance of holding the Yazoo… [but] ordered Captain Brown to move at once with his steamer and act as his judgment should dictate."

Van Dorn hoped that Brown could "sweep the river" below Vicksburg and head for toward New Orleans and even Mobile.

Leaving Van Dorn, Lieutenant Read spent the rest of his day on one of the bluffs overlooking the river upstream to see what the *Arkansas* would face. He saw "thirteen heavy sloops of war, mounting tremendous batteries" anchored near the east bank. Davis's thirty or so ironclads and six or eight rams were close to the west bank, with the mortar boats downstream.

While Read was noting the odds against his ship and probably concluding that the *Arkansas*'s chances depended on surprising the enemy, the log of the ram *Lancaster* noted that two Confederate deserters came in with word that the *Arkansas* would come down the Yazoo on the night of July 14.[77]

Read left Vicksburg at dark and rode most of the night to rejoin his ship. The *Arkansas* did indeed head downriver on July 14.

In its brief life from July 14 to August 6, the *Arkansas* made only two voyages—from Yazoo City to Vicksburg, and from Vicksburg to near Baton Rouge. Her engines, or boilers, did not function properly either time. On the way down the Yazoo, one of the boilers leaked steam into the forward magazine. Brown had to tie up, bring out all the powder onto the riverbank and spread it out onto tarpaulins to let it dry in the sun. In another close call, the ship almost lost its stack to a branch hanging low over the water.[78] But the ship resumed its voyage and later tied up for the night.

She set out again at first light on the fifteenth. "As the sun rose clear and fiery we saw, a few miles ahead under full steam, three Federal vessels in line approaching." Three against one were favorable odds compared to what lay ahead, but Brown feared that any engagement on the Yazoo would cost him the element of surprise on the Mississippi. The Union ships, led by Commander Henry Walke, an old friend of Brown's, were the ironclad *Carondelet*, which was Walke's ship, the ram *Queen of the West* and the wooden gunboat *Tyler*. "This was not a good moment for Union ships to explore the Yazoo."[79]

Lieutenant Brown ordered his crew to prepare the ship for battle.

> *The guns were loaded and cast loose, their tackles in the hands of willing seamen…primers in the vents; locks thrown back and lanyards in the hands of the gun captains; the decks sprinkled with sand and tourniquets*

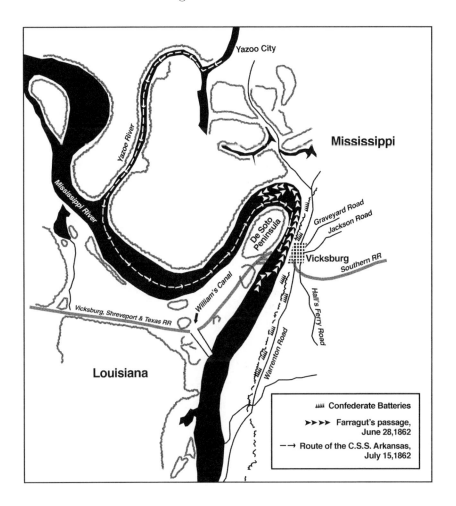

The River at Vicksburg. July 15, 1862. *By Marshall Hudson.*

and bandages at hand, tubs filled with fresh water were between the guns, and down in the berth deck were the surgeons with their bright instruments, stimulants and lint, while along the passageways stood rows of men to pass powder, shell and shot and all was quiet save the dull thump of the propellers.[80]

The stillness of a hot early morning ended abruptly. The great saga of the *Arkansas* had begun. A Confederate infantryman in Vicksburg,

William Dixon, remembered being awakened "by the thundering of a 'war dog' up the river."[81] Brown went for the *Carondelet*, not firing his bow guns, which would reduce his speed, but intending to ram her and then turn at close quarters and give her a broadside. The *Carondelet* escaped being rammed but ran aground. As the *Arkansas* closed in, the *Tyler* tried to save her, laying down a heavy fire. Brown suffered a "serious contusion on the head," and then a sharpshooter on the *Tyler* grazed his head with a minie ball. Brown would not be denied; he brought the *Arkansas* alongside his victim: "Our port broadside caused her to heel to port and then roll back so deeply as to take water over her deck." Brown had fired at thirty feet. "We left him hanging in the willows," he wrote.[82] He then turned on the other two ships, which "very properly took advantage of a speed double ours to gain the shelter of their fleet."[83] In the downriver chase, heading for the Mississippi River, the *Arkansas* punished the *Tyler* severely. It was a foretaste of what lay ahead. "The *Tyler*'s decks presented a shocking spectacle…she had been hulled eleven times, besides being cut up by grape…her decks were literally running with blood."[84] Brown's two pilots were both wounded, one mortally. As the chase neared its end, the two Union ships pulled farther ahead of the *Arkansas*, further jeopardizing Brown's hope of surprising the main fleet. When the *Arkansas* finally came into the Mississippi, there were, for the moment, no Union ships in sight. The *Arkansas* continued churning ahead, while Brown took advantage of the lull to inspect his ship. The stack was riddled, reducing his speed. Below, her boiler pressure was at 120 pounds and dropping. The temperature was 120 degrees and rising. First Lieutenant Henry K. Stevens, Brown's executive officer, was firing the engines, rotating his stokers in shifts of fifteen minutes.

When Brown came back on deck, the enemy was in sight. The Confederates saw "a forest of masts and smokestacks—ships, rams, ironclads and other gunboats on the left side and ordinary river steamers and bomb vessels along the right…in every direction, except astern, our eyes rested on our enemies."[85]

Amazingly, surprise was still on Brown's side. "The *Arkansas* had surprised the combined fleets."[86] Only a few Union crewmen, on different ships, had heard the firing and prepared for battle. Most thought that their ships in the Yazoo must be dueling with shore batteries.[87] One Union officer wrote: "All was confusion. Not anyone seemed prepared, nor had they steam up enough to alter their position."[88]

Aboard the Union ships, crews scrambled into action, while the *Arkansas* pushed forward into point-blank range. The first shots woke up Farragut, who, to the amusement of his men, appeared on deck wearing only his nightgown.[89] "We made for Farragut's fleet and gave them the best we had at close quarters. Our guns were blazing destruction and defiance in every direction, fighting our way right and left," Lieutenant Read remembered.[90]

According to the log of the *Lancaster*, she was the first to feel the *Arkansas*'s tremendous hitting power. At a range of one hundred yards, a sixty-four-pound ball came through the ram's bulwarks and eight feet of coal to tear off the top three feet of the "steam drum," i.e., the boiler. The impact and the scalding steam killed or wounded nearly ten men. One man, scalded nearly to death, jumped into the river, where he was shot. Another, whose legs and one arm had been torn off, mercifully died in a few minutes. The *Lancaster* took three hits from other Union vessels downstream. Grape and canister rounds littered the deck. "The *Lancaster* is disabled, being shot all to pieces," the log concluded.[91]

Brown wrote, "I had the most lively realization of having steamed into a volcano." It was worse than running a gauntlet. Brown had the feeling that the *Arkansas* was surrounded. It gave him one advantage: he could "fire without the fear of hitting a friend or missing an enemy." There was little or no wind, and smoke from the guns hung in the air. Gunners on both sides often fired at gun flashes, even though the ranges were very close. Brown remembered scoring a direct hit on a Union ram and seeing its crew in the water—"brave fellows struggling in the water under a stream of missiles intended for us."[92]

At one point, the *Arkansas* took a full broadside from the USS *Richmond*. "Eight hundred and eighty-two pounds of metal…the *Arkansas* continued without having apparently suffered any crippling damage. [Union Commander James] Alden and his officers shook their heads in disbelief. According to the books, no vessel afloat was supposed to withstand such a fearful blow."[93]

The lone ship gave as good as she got. In heat like that of a furnace, with a steady succession of sledgehammer blows to the ship's armor, strong enough to inflict concussions, "each man carried out his task as if he seemed to believe the safety of the vessel depended on his own actions."[94]

By the time Brown neared Vicksburg, he had no choice but to put in under the protection of the batteries. His boiler pressure and speed had fallen severely. Two eleven-inch shells had pierced the ship's armor. The engine room was filled with smoke and was hot as a furnace, and there was more blood on the gun deck than the sand could absorb.[95]

Van Dorn watched from the courthouse cupola, with Breckinridge and a few others, as the ship drew close. According to one observer, "When it came in sight of us Captain Brown was standing on the bow waving his cap in one hand and a Confederate flag in the other."[96] If this was indeed Brown, it was a remarkable achievement. One of his officers wrote that "Captain Brown was twice knocked off his platform, stunned, his marine glass was broken in his hand, and he received a wound on his temple." The vessel and its crew paid a heavy price. Brown reported, "Our smokestack was so shot to pieces that we lost steam and could not use our vessel as a ram. We were otherwise cut up as we engaged at close quarters."[97] Lieutenant L.D. Young, in Breckinridge's Orphan Brigade, was on the landing. He wrote in 1918, "We could see the monster (so to speak) in her grim and battered condition with numerous holes in her smokestack and a large piece torn out of her cast prow."[98] According to one account, the colors had been shot away, but Brown certainly did return to the platform at some point.

Van Dorn and those with him rushed from the courthouse to the landing through a cheering crowd, onto the ship, to congratulate the crew.[99] Van Dorn later wrote that Brown had "immortalized his single vessel, himself, and the heroes under his command."[100] Those who came aboard could not, of course, have heard what the crew had endured: "A din…nearly unimaginable as hundreds of sledge hammer blows were delivered to the armor plate by cannon fire that was literally continuous."[101] Many of the crew suffered concussions and bleeding from the nose and ears, as well as deafness, temporary or permanent. But what they could see was horrifying even to hardened soldiers. Gift described "a great heap of mangled slain, rivulets of blood running away."[102] "The scene around the gun deck…was ghastly. Blood and brains bespattered everything; while arms, legs and several headless trunks were strewn about." In all, Brown's casualties so far on July 15 came to sixteen killed and twenty wounded. Union losses were sixteen killed, fifty wounded and ten missing.[103]

The *Arkansas*'s voyage was over, but not her ordeal. Brown first moved the ship from the landing to a coaling dock. While the ship was coaling, at least one of Farragut's big ships opened fire, landing shells in the water close enough to sprinkle down the coal dust. Brown then moved his ship back to the landing.

Farragut was determined to destroy the ship that had sailed through his fleets. Late that afternoon, he ordered another tremendous bombardment. Some of Davis's ships came down to join in. At that time of day, Union ships were silhouetted against the setting sun, giving the gunners good targets. The *Arkansas*, however, was difficult to see. General Williams wrote, "She is very low in the water and about the color of the river bank. The rebel monster could not be seen."[104] An army quartermaster on board one of Farragut's ships thought that the *Arkansas* must have been hidden behind a wharf boat.[105] Nevertheless, either the *Hartford* or the *Richmond* sent a one-hundred-pound wrought-iron ball through the armor into the engine room, killing one man, destroying Dr. Washington's dispensary and lodging in the opposite wall. But the *Arkansas* survived. Brown saluted his officers and men as "worthy of the American name."[106] "Glorious for the navy, and glorious for her heroic commander, officers and men," Van Dorn wrote the next day.[107]

The ship altered the strategic situation at Vicksburg, bringing the siege to a turning point. By fighting through the two fleets and anchoring downstream of them, the *Arkansas* reinforced Farragut's conviction that taking Vicksburg was beyond the navy's power.[108] With the river level falling and the *Arkansas* between him and the mortar boats—and New Orleans—Farragut declared, "We were all caught unprepared for him, but we must go down and destroy him."[109] If he could not, he had no choice but to abandon the siege. The canal had proved a fruitless, costly failure. The infantry and the ships' crews were exhausted, with many falling sick. In the extreme July heat, dysentery and heat exhaustion alike often proved fatal.

At sunrise on July 16, Farragut began a bombardment that Lieutenant Young still recalled fifty-six years later in the midst of news from the Great War. He wrote that it was "terrifying…never been equaled unless it has occurred…on the Western Front or at the Dardanelles…The air was literally hardened with ascending and descending shells from the upper and lower fleets…illuminated the surroundings for miles…every color of the rainbow…balloon shaped clouds of smoke…not all the wonders and terrors of war are young."[110]

Over the next six days, Farragut attempted to destroy the *Arkansas*. Brown, Van Dorn, Smith and the surviving crew countered by moving the ship from one landing to another, bringing infantry up close to the banks in case the Federals made an attempt to board her.

Farragut's most determined and nearly successful attempt came on July 22, when the USS *Essex* and the *Queen of the West* attempted to ram and board her. By that time, the *Arkansas* had only a skeleton crew—many had been injured or were ill, and Van Dorn had been unable—inexplicably—to get new volunteers to Brown. Men did volunteer. Captain Hoole, of the Hudson Battery, had thirteen men ready to board the *Arkansas*. But in a Civil War version of a military snafu, they never could get aboard. Angrily, Hoole wrote that they were "obliged to return to camp without having accomplished anything."[111] Eventually, President Davis got involved, asking Governor Pettus if he could not help Captain Brown to get an adequate crew.[112] The number of volunteers who came aboard, if any, is unclear. In any event, Brown thought that a Federal boarding party would have a good chance of overpowering the small crew and taking the ship. As the *Essex* drew near, the *Arkansas* opened fire. The undermanned crew raced from gun to gun, to load, run out, train and fire each in turn. As the *Essex* came on, the *Arkansas* swung its bow around, showing itself "thin as a wedge." The *Essex* glanced off, running down the *Arkansas*'s side. Brown said it was no more than a "nudge." The fire from the shore batteries was so severe that after a second miss, the *Essex* backed off. There was no organized rush to board the *Arkansas*.[113]

CSS *Arkansas* flag. The *Arkansas*'s flag (17'1" x 8'2") was said to have been captured by one of the *Queen of the West*'s engineers, a civilian. The engineer's descendants donated this flag to the Port Columbus National Civil War Naval Museum in Columbus, Georgia, in 1999. The museum credits the flag as historically authentic. *Photograph by Bob Price.*

After this failure, Farragut made ready to return to New Orleans. Brown wrote later, "If the *Arkansas* could not be destroyed, the siege must be raised, for fifty ships, more or less, could not keep perpetual steam to confine one little ten gun vessel with her conceded control of six miles of the Mississippi River."[114] Brown came out on the twenty-third showing fight but intending only to force the Federals to get steam up. Once they had, he returned to shore.[115] The next day, Van Dorn reported: "The whole of the lower fleet and all the troops have disappeared down the river." Three days later, Governor Pettus informed Richmond that "all of the enemy's boats and troops have left Vicksburg."[116] Van Dorn, Smith and Brown had won. The first Vicksburg campaign was over.

With Vicksburg safe, Van Dorn began to think in strategic terms. First, Vicksburg's defenses must be strengthened, especially on the land side. "Nothing can be accomplished by the enemy unless they bring overwhelming numbers of troops. This must be anticipated."[117]

Next, he "resolved to strike a blow before he [the enemy] had time to organize and mature a new scheme of assault."[118] Van Dorn believed that the summer's successes had earned him the strategic initiative, and he meant to use it. He believed that if he could recover Baton Rouge, or take Port Hudson, both below the mouth of the Red River, he could "seal off" the stretch of river between either point and Vicksburg. This, in theory, would allow for supplies from the Trans-Mississippi to be brought down the Red River and then up to Vicksburg. "It was a matter of great necessity to us that the navigation of Red River should be opened as high as Vicksburg."[119]

Baton Rouge, about forty miles below the Red River, and Port Hudson, about ten miles below, were obvious targets. Port Hudson was on higher ground than Baton Rouge, and it also had a railroad connection with Clinton, nineteen miles distant. But Baton Rouge was a state capital, temptingly close to New Orleans. General Thomas Williams now held Baton Rouge, with seven infantry regiments, four batteries of artillery and as many as ten ships.

Van Dorn knew his resources were limited. Illness had thinned his ranks, as well as Farragut's. President Davis had no reinforcements to send him. Van Dorn decided, therefore, to go ahead with what he had—Breckinridge's division, reinforced with Ruggles's troops from Tangipahoa, Louisiana. Breckinridge left Vicksburg on July 27. By the time he was in position to attack, his command's strength was down to about 2,800 and falling fast. He believed the garrison was

> not less than 5,000 men, and that the ground was commanded by three gunboats lying in the river…I determined not to make the attack unless we could be relieved from the fire of the fleet. Accordingly I telegraphed to [Van Dorn] the condition and number of the troops and the reported strength of the enemy, but said I would undertake to capture the garrison if the Arkansas could be sent down to clear the river…[Van Dorn] promptly answered that the Arkansas would be ready to co-operate at daylight on Tuesday, August 5.[120]

Breckinridge believed that his men could push the Federals right to the water's edge. If the Arkansas could sink or drive away the gunboats, his men would not have to cope with the firepower, or the psychological impact, of an enemy they could not reach. Breckinridge had seen firsthand at the Battle of Shiloh the effect that gunboats could have on infantry. The problem was to get the *Arkansas* to Baton Rouge to support his attack.

The *Arkansas* was still at Vicksburg. Mechanics and engineers from Jackson and even Mobile were at work on the necessary repairs. Brown was recuperating from his wounds in Grenada; First Lieutenant Stevens was temporarily in command. Brown had complete confidence in Stevens, who, he wrote, "had had much harder work to do than any other officer on board and he has done it well."[121] Moreover, he thought Stevens was "a religious soldier, of the Stonewall Jackson type." He left Stevens with orders, he wrote later, not to take the ship out anywhere until the repairs were complete.[122] Lieutenant Read believed that, in deference to Breckinridge, Stevens decided to take the ship down before the mechanics had finished or Brown had returned. "As no Confederate could refuse to comply with the wish of one so universally loved and respected as General Breckinridge, Stevens consented to go."[123]

Van Dorn, however, is usually blamed for putting persistent and irresistible pressure on Stevens, overriding Brown and even conniving with Commodore Lynch, a Confederate naval officer then in Jackson, to send the *Arkansas* to her doom. Van Dorn settled the issue himself, exactly as Breckinridge had put it: "To insure the success of the plan I ordered the *Arkansas* to co-operate with the land forces."[124]

In any event, Brown wrote that when he learned the ship was going downstream, he got up out of his sickbed and rushed to the Grenada depot, "where I threw myself on the mailbags of the first passing train to Jackson." When he arrived, hoping for a fast connection or even a special train to Vicksburg, he learned that he was already too late. The *Arkansas* had gone.[125]

The *Arkansas* left Vicksburg at 2:00 a.m. on August 4, bound for Baton Rouge. Breckinridge attacked early on August 5. The Battle of Baton Rouge was a murderous one. There were over eight hundred casualties, including General Williams. Breckinridge fought his way close to the water's edge and might have taken Baton Rouge if the joint operation had been made to work. But it was not to be. The *Arkansas* almost made it to Baton Rouge, in spite of no fewer than five engine failures between August 4 and mid-morning on August 6. After the engineers had rectified the fourth engine failure, Stevens was convinced his ship was ready to do its part. With her old foe, the USS *Essex*, and several other ships bearing down on him, Stevens increased his engine speed—and the starboard engine failed. The proud but frustrated vessel swung around and went aground with its stern toward its enemy. Lieutenant Read went into action, ordering his gun crews to open fire from the stern. The Union flotilla commander, Commodore W.D. Porter, claimed that Stevens would have never destroyed his own ship and that he, Porter, deserved the credit. He claimed fourteen direct hits on the *Arkansas*. Even other Federal accounts found his claim dubious.[126] But Stevens, with a heavy heart, decided that he had no choice but to abandon ship, destroy her and save the crew. Read continued firing until he heard the order to abandon ship.[127] Lieutenant Gift saw Stevens's "look of anguish" as he prepared the ship for its final voyage.[128] It was no ignominious scuttling. The crew loaded the ship's guns, Stevens lit fires and all jumped ashore to push her out into the strong current. The fire reached at least some of the guns, which exploded as if in defiance. The flames then reached the powder magazine. Van Dorn (who was not there) wrote, "With every gun shotted, our flag floating from her bow and not a man on board, the *Arkansas* bore down upon the enemy and gave him battle. The guns were discharged as the flames reached them, and when her last shot was fired the explosion of her magazine ended the brief but glorious career of the *Arkansas*. 'It was beautiful,' said Lieutenant Stevens, while the tears stood in his eyes, 'to see her abandoned by commander and crew and dedicated to sacrifice, fighting the battle on her own hook.'"[129]

The ship's "biographer," Tom Parrish, wrote a fitting epitaph: "Though she had ended with a bang and not with a whimper, her iron armor sank like a stone dropped into a well, leaving not a trace behind except the rending pain of memory."[130]

When Breckinridge learned the fate of the *Arkansas*, he halted his attack and withdrew. But he had no intention of backtracking to Vicksburg with his mission unfulfilled. Port Hudson presented him with an opportunity to fulfill the mission. Van Dorn and Breckinridge both saw the chance. By the time Van Dorn's order to occupy Port Hudson reached Breckinridge, he had already decided to act. Ruggles's troops began moving into Port Hudson on August 15. "The portal through which steamboats plying the waters of the Red River" could enter the Mississippi and head upstream for Vicksburg was now in Confederate hands.[131]

The great Union victories of the spring and summer—taking New Orleans, Baton Rouge, Natchez and then Memphis—cost the Confederacy dearly. The loss of three unfinished ironclads and the hard-hitting *Arkansas* compounded the damage. Union control of the entire length of the river, severing the Trans-Mississippi from the rest of the Confederacy, seemed imminent. But Vicksburg had held, and Port Hudson was now a strong Confederate bastion below the mouth of the Red River. Port Hudson undoubtedly protected Trans-Mississippi commerce. Unfortunately, there is little statistical data to show exactly how beneficial Port Hudson was to "sealing off" the river upstream to Vicksburg. One "statistical fragment" shows that on January 20, 1863, the steamboat *T.R. Hine* docked at Vicksburg with an enormous cargo of salt, flour, lard, bacon and hogs. The Trans-Mississippi sources of supply were rich, especially the saltworks at New Iberia, Louisiana. But as always in Confederate logistical history, storage and transport difficulties worked against the distribution of the resources available. The Southern Railroad could move as much as two hundred tons a day from Vicksburg to Jackson, but getting supplies to Vicksburg was becoming more and more difficult. As early as October 1862, Governor Pettus described to President Davis how difficult it was to get salt from New Iberia across the river to Vicksburg.[132]

As for Vicksburg, Van Dorn, Smith and Brown had turned back the navy. But Van Dorn knew the enemy was coming again, in far greater strength, on the land side. He had bought Vicksburg time—but time proved to be short. The next Vicksburg campaign did not await the spring of 1863; it came in the fall and winter of 1862. By then, Van Dorn was no longer "our bold young leader." His career and reputation had taken a drastic turn for the worse. In October, the *Memphis Daily Appeal* linked him with Lovell and the infamous Gideon J. Pillow, saying, "It is the solemn duty of the President to remove these generals from their commands."[133]

Chapter 3

General Van Dorn and Colonel Murphy

Charges Dismissed

In the early spring of 1862, the Confederacy had been close to defeat. But by the late summer, the Confederacy was closer to victory and independence than at any time in its brief history. The successful defense of Vicksburg had been part of a "military miracle." It was most obvious in Virginia, where General Robert E. Lee's Army of Northern Virginia had saved Richmond from McClellan, defeated Pope at Manassas and, in early September, as bands played "Maryland, My Maryland," crossed the Potomac. General Braxton Bragg's Army of Tennessee (as it was soon to be designated) was already on the move from Tupelo to Chattanooga by rail (via Mobile and Atlanta) and then on into Kentucky. Earl Van Dorn, as commander of the Department of Southern Mississippi and East Louisiana, had a secondary but important role in Bragg's plans. In cooperation with General Sterling Price's Army of the West, he was to prevent Union forces in West Tennessee from marching to the aid of Union forces contending with Bragg in Kentucky.[134]

President Davis impressed upon Van Dorn the necessity of close cooperation with Price. "Your rank makes you the commander," he told Van Dorn, cautioning him at the same time to "have due care to the safety of Vicksburg, Port Hudson, &c."[135] Van Dorn believed he could accomplish both objectives—holding Union forces in Tennessee and taking due care of Vicksburg—by recovering Corinth. Although Price attacked Union General William Rosecrans at Iuka before Van Dorn joined him, the two combined their forces at Ripley on September 28. Together, they had twenty-two thousand men, a force nearly as large as General William Rosecrans's garrison at Corinth. They had a fair chance of success.[136]

However, it was not to be. The Battle of Corinth was a bloody Confederate defeat. Van Dorn's casualties were nearly 5,000, including 2,102 missing or captured. Most of the killed and wounded fell in fierce, but futile, uncoordinated attacks on strong Federal positions. Confederate Brigadier General Dabney H. Maury reported that "our ranks had been fearfully thinned…we felt how bootless had been their sacrifice, and how different the result would have been had our charge upon the works been supported. The utmost depression prevailed throughout the army."[137]

In Richmond, Josiah Gorgas, the chief of ordnance for the Confederacy, related that the president "was much depressed and said we had been out-generaled."[138] President Davis had seen trouble coming, citing "the want of co-intelligence and co-operation." He had, in fact, already sent Lieutenant General John C. Pemberton to Jackson to take command of Van Dorn's department in the event of a disaster. On October 12, Pemberton took over.[139] The president wanted Van Dorn to remain in Mississippi but as a subordinate in a department he had formerly commanded.[140]

It was the second bloody defeat Van Dorn had suffered and the low point in his career. He was staggered and humiliated. "I attacked Corinth and took it," he protested on October 12, "but could not hold it."[141] He was more realistic and accurate a week later: "The attempt at Corinth has failed, and in consequence I am condemned and have been superseded in my command. In my zeal for my country I may have ventured too far with inadequate means."[142] This is fair enough. Van Dorn is not alone in this or any other war in overreaching. But in addition to the terrible defeat, Van Dorn now had to contend with rumors and allegations of private misconduct. On October 5, a soldier in the 43rd Mississippi wrote in a letter home:

Van Dorn I hear had been having a good time in Holly Springs for the few days before the march on Corinth. 'Tis said that he was a regular bender, this is hearsay…I am inclined to believe it…He has done our cause more injury in the past two years than he can repair in a lifetime… The army of the west this morning is a disorganized mass and won't follow Van Dorn at but a slow pace—they are heartedly tired of him.[143]

Another letter reached the president, dated October 7, from citizens in Holly Springs: "We believe from indisputable evidence and we think the belief is general that the habits of Gens. Van Dorn and Lovell are too intemperate to warrant their being retained in command of a large army. We look only for disasters under them, we therefore suggest they may be relieved and men of sobriety put in their places."[144]

Allegations of scandal and impropriety could not be quelled once coupled with military defeat. Van Dorn felt the sting. He thanked one loyal friend, who "had not believed the slander against my character…I thought I had no friends…do not believe all that you hear. I shall come out of this as proudly as you could wish and I shall be vindicated."[145]

November brought even worse tidings. In the bitter aftermath of Corinth, Brigadier General John S. Bowen, who had commanded a division in Lovell's corps at Corinth, accused Van Dorn of professional misconduct. He charged that Van Dorn "did utterly fail and neglect to discharge his duties as a general commanding an army." He charged in particular that Van Dorn had not provided himself with a proper map of the approaches and plan of the works attacked, that he did not consult an engineer officer nor did he reconnoiter before the attack, that he provided his troops with no commissary stores and that the attack was made in a hasty and disorderly manner, under the mistaken notion that surprise could still be achieved against an enemy with whom he had been in contact for the previous thirty-six hours.[146]

When Van Dorn learned of Bowen's charges, he may have asked for a full court-martial. President Davis wrote to him on November 4, saying that the matter gave him "great pain," but that a court of inquiry was preferable to a court-martial.[147] Lieutenant General Pemberton ordered the court to convene at Abbeville on November 15. The court detail included Major General Sterling Price as president and Brigadier Generals Lloyd Tilghman and Dabney Maury. Van Dorn introduced Colonel Wright as his advisor.

After a week of testimony, Van Dorn made a very lengthy closing statement. He cited his successful defense of Vicksburg and warned again of a stronger Union effort sure to follow in the next year. He defended the attack on Corinth as a "spoiling operation" on Vicksburg's behalf, as well as the best thing he could have done to help Bragg in Kentucky. He concluded by turning from the specific accusations to a defense of his character, denouncing the "clandestine and cowardly falsehoods, sent on electric currents to the President at Richmond and by wholesale and loud mouthed calumny scattered over my native State." He finished with a heartfelt flourish: "I am a Mississippian by birth. The ashes of my parents repose in this soil…I struck for her as I would strike for wife or child."

On November 28, Pemberton announced that "every allegation made against [Van Dorn] is fully disproved."[148] Van Dorn had won. To mark his victory he is said to have compiled, printed and mailed out one thousand pamphlets bearing the news.[149]

Van Dorn had cleared his name as a soldier, but the attacks on his character continued. Senator James Phelan of Mississippi wrote on December 9 to President Davis that the atmosphere in Mississippi was "dense with horrid narratives of his negligence, whoring, and drunkenness…an acquittal by a court-martial of angels would not relieve him of the charge."[150]

The president already had before him Van Dorn's letter (December 8) announcing his acquittal. Van Dorn went on, unfortunately, to admit that he was known as a "soldier and libertine" in stories that went back to the summer in Vicksburg. It was alleged that he had seduced a young girl, but "as a Christian man and before my God I declare that it is false…I never seduced any young lady in my life…with the exception of my wife. I have never had intercourse with any woman, I believe, who was not alike accessible to others…" He admitted to "indiscretions…thoughtlessness and folly—or pleasantries as they may be called," claiming that "I have been stabbed in the back…I am unfortunately not a good Christian—but I am not a Seducer, nor a drunkard…it *was* my pride that I was a soldier without fear and without reproach." In closing, he asked for transfer from Mississippi. "Remove me any where, so it be in the field where our enemies are."[151] Davis must have blanched at this letter, but he wisely decided not to move Van Dorn. The general would remain in Mississippi and was, in fact, only twelve days removed from the high point of his career, his great moment of triumph at Holly Springs.

There was a second officer for whom the fall of 1862 was a time of troubles, an officer whose destiny was interwoven with Van Dorn and Holly Springs. Union Colonel Robert Creighton Murphy (1827–1888) was born in Chillicothe, Ohio. He earned a law degree from Miami University of Ohio. He served on the Mexican Boundary Commission and then was American consul in Shanghai. Difficulties there with American merchants and perhaps alcohol forced him to resign in 1857. He returned to the St. Croix Valley in Wisconsin, where he managed investments. When the war broke out, he was appointed colonel of the 8th Wisconsin Volunteer Infantry. By the spring of 1862, he commanded a brigade in General William S. Rosecrans's Army of the Mississippi. His trouble began just before the Battle of Iuka, September 19, 1862, the prelude to Van Dorn's defeat at Corinth. When General Price moved on Iuka, General Rosecrans ordered Murphy to hold Iuka at least until valuable commissary and medical stores could be brought out. "For God's sake don't skedaddle…look at your orders."[152] Murphy did not hold Iuka long enough, and a large amount of stores was neither burned nor taken out. Rosecrans, furious, placed Murphy under arrest on September 14, writing, "I think extreme fright and want of judgment of Colonel Murphy so manifest as to need no comment."[153] Rosecrans was blunt: Murphy "ran away from the enemy…before an inferior force…without making a stand, and…did disobey said orders and did shamefully abandon said post…with result that the supplies were lost."[154] "We captured a good many stores," wrote Private Robert Banks. "The Yankees live like fighting cocks."[155]

A court-martial, with General John A. McArthur presiding, heard the charges. On September 25, Murphy explained his actions with a welter of mitigating and apparently plausible excuses. The court dismissed the charges. A surgeon then submitted his opinion that the colonel would

General Van Dorn and Colonel Murphy

Robert C. Murphy, 1827–1888. His dismissal from the army was dated from the day of the raid on Holly Springs. He tried without success to clear his name. *Photograph courtesy of Massachusetts Commandery Military Order of the Loyal Legion and the U.S. Army Military History Institute.*

benefit from a leave of thirty days because of "chronic inflammation of the liver."

Major General U.S. Grant was, by then, head of the Department of the Tennessee and was planning his campaign to take Vicksburg. Grant took a more forgiving and benign view of Murphy's conduct and fitness for future command. He thought Murphy had done well enough merely to avoid capture. On December 12, he installed Murphy as commander of the District of the Tallahatchie, guarding the line of the Mississippi Central Railroad from Coldwater to Oxford.[156] Murphy established his headquarters in Holly Springs, on the line of the Mississippi Central.

Holly Springs and the Mississippi Central Railroad

Mary Ann Loughborough, the wife of a Confederate major, described Holly Springs, Mississippi, as she saw it in 1862: "With its wide verandahed houses, its pleasant gardens, wide streets and hospitable homes [it] is one of the most pleasant Southern towns."[157] Her description remains true today. As in 1862, the tracks of the Mississippi Central Railroad skirt the eastern edge of town. The postwar Illinois Central Railroad passenger station stands today where the wartime depot stood. In 1862, Depot Street led from the depot to the town square. It does today, but it is now named Van Dorn Avenue. Just as surely as the Mississippi River brought the war to Vicksburg, the Mississippi Central Railroad brought it to Holly Springs.

Marshall County was formed in 1836, and Holly Springs was incorporated the next year. By 1850, the county, known as the "Empire County," had the largest population of any in the state—14,271 whites and free blacks and 15,147 slaves. Holly Springs, with about 3,500 inhabitants, was known as the "Capital of North Mississippi." Cotton was truly king here. In 1860, King Cotton's domain was 128,000 acres, and his yield was nearly fifty thousand bales a year. In 1852, the king had summoned his steed—the iron horse—what one writer called "Holly Springs's supreme achievement, the Mississippi Central."[158]

Holly Springs and the Mississippi Central Railroad

The Mississippi Central Railroad still comes south from Grand Junction, Tennessee, through Holly Springs but only as far south as Oxford, Mississippi. *Photograph by Garrie Colhoun.*

The Mississippi Central grew in fits and starts. Its initial aim was to connect Canton, Mississippi, just over twenty miles north of Jackson, Mississippi, with Jackson, Tennessee, some 250 miles farther north. Track layers (mostly slaves; investors could purchase shares with cash or labor) got no farther north than the line of the Memphis & Charleston, running east to Corinth. From Grand Junction on the Memphis & Charleston, forty miles east of Memphis, the Mississippi Central could reach points farther south: Davis' Mill, Lamar, Hudsonville on the Coldwater River, Holly Springs, Lumpkin's Mill, Abbeville on the Tallahatchie River, Oxford, Water Valley, Coffeeville and Grenada, just south of the Yalobusha River. The railroad's founding fathers—Walter Goodman, Harvey Walter and A.M. West—were Holly Springs men. After the line's right of way reached Holly Springs on November 11,

1853, their town became the railroad's most important town and de facto headquarters.

After the right of way came the wood-burning engines with their tall drive wheels and huge smokestacks. In 1855, the *Vicksburg Weekly Whig* reported that "two beautiful and highly polished locomotives for the Mississippi Central arrived in Memphis, named the *H.M. Walter* and the *Joseph Collins*…the engineer fired up the latter and let the screaming whistle proclaim 'The Mississippi Central is born.'"[159]

Holly Springs already had a history of iron foundries, beginning with small establishments in the 1840s and 1850s. But by the end of the decade, a truly large establishment had grown up—the Jones-McElwaine Iron Foundry. In 1859, it produced 1,350 tons of iron castings, including residential grillwork, balconies, capitals, plows and rails for the Mississippi Central.[160]

In January 1860, track layers completed the line between Water Valley and Grenada. Seven hundred people saw the ceremonial spike driven home at a festive occasion at Winona.[161]

Overshadowing the coming together of the Mississippi Central in 1860 was the coming apart of the Union. Two months after secession, riders and newspapers quickly spread the news of Sumter across the state. The war came, slowly but surely, to Holly Springs. The Jones-McElwaine Foundry won a contract from the new government to manufacture and/or repair rifles and other articles of war. In February 1862, the Confederate government bought the foundry, now an important armory. In the fall of 1862, the government moved all its machinery from Holly Springs to a more secure location farther south, in Macon, Georgia.[162]

On October 19, something very much like war came to the Mississippi Central at Duck Hill, just north of Winona. A head-on collision between a troop train and a regularly scheduled passenger train claimed nearly forty lives and left a stretch of the line just south of the depot looking like a battlefield.[163] A memorial cemetery next to the tracks in Duck Hill today recalls the horrendous accident.

In November, the threat to Vicksburg Van Dorn had foreseen materialized. Major General Ulysses S. Grant began an advance along the line of the Mississippi Railroad. Grant's Army of the Tennessee soon

The grave of Colonel
J.L. Autry in Hill Crest
Cemetery, Holly Springs.
Photograph by Garrie Colhoun.

reached Holly Springs. One Union soldier called it "a fine town, best I have seen in Mississippi."[164] Soldiers of the 109th Illinois also liked Holly Springs, saying it reminded them of home, reported James Evans in the *Jonesboro Gazette* on November 22, 1862. But Evans also reported, "The graveyards are crowded with fresh graves, filled by the instigation of this terrible rebellion. Many of their resting places are marked by beautiful monuments with touching inscriptions."[165]

Among those Confederate graves with touching inscriptions, visitors today can see the grave of Lieutenant J.L. Autry, who had defied Captain Lee's demand for the surrender of Vicksburg. Autry was killed at the Battle of Murfreesboro, Tennessee, on the last day of 1862. The inscription on his monument records that Lieutenant Autry's father, Micajah, was no better at surrendering than his son; he had died at the Alamo in 1836.

Chapter 5

Grant

On the Square in Oxford

In the fall of 1862, Major General Ulysses S. Grant was ready to mount the second campaign against Vicksburg. He had about fifty-six thousand men in the Department of West Tennessee, guarding its railroads and lines of communication. General Henry Halleck, who had replaced Grant as field commander after Shiloh and had shown no interest in supporting Farragut at Vicksburg, was now in Washington as Lincoln's general in chief. On October 16, Grant became head of a larger department with great resources—the Department of the Tennessee. The Confederates in North Mississippi seemed weak and disorganized after Corinth; Grant did not intend to wait until spring to move. His goal was to take Vicksburg.

Two days before Grant took command of his department, Van Dorn gave up command of his. The new departmental commander was General John C. Pemberton. Van Dorn retained command of what became known as the Army of North Mississippi, about twenty-four thousand men, with his headquarters in Holly Springs. Pemberton established his headquarters at Jackson. He preferred administrative work there to command in the field. There was a pressing need for such work, and Pemberton did it well.[166] He devoted most of his time and skill to solving what were already severe logistical problems. However, Pemberton did

Ulysses S. Grant, 1822–1885. Victor at Fort Henry, Fort Donelson and Shiloh; took Vicksburg in 1863 and Richmond in 1865. President of the United States, 1869–77. *From* The Photographic History of the Civil War in Ten Volumes, *ed. Francis Trevelyan Miller, vol. 10.*

keep a train with steam up to be ready to leave for Vicksburg or Holly Springs at a moment's notice.[167]

Van Dorn urged Pemberton on October 16, "Come here as soon as possible…you cannot be here too soon to prepare for action…The enemy in West Tennessee is about 45,000 strong, and re-inforcements daily arriving. You had better get some of Holmes' troops, if you would save Mississippi."[168] Lieutenant General Theophilus H. Holmes (1804–1880) commanded the Trans-Mississippi district beginning in October 1862.

His headquarters were in Little Rock. Pemberton, however, doubted that any reinforcements from Arkansas were coming over the river. For the moment, he did not want to leave Jackson. Pemberton ordered Van Dorn to withdraw below the Tallahatchie if Grant advanced.[169]

As October drew to a close, Grant planned his advance. In order to take Vicksburg from the land side, he faced a serious logistical problem: how to supply his army in North Mississippi. He could *begin* the campaign with wagon trains and foraging parties, but as he moved deeper into Mississippi, he intended to rely on the Mississippi Central Railroad. The railroad would be his line of advance—to Grenada and then to Jackson or Vicksburg—and his line of supply. Guerrilla activity and a shortage of railway equipment probably ruled out Memphis as a supply source. Supplies would come to the Mississippi Central by rail from Jackson, Tennessee, and be stockpiled first at Grand Junction and then later at some point on the railroad farther south.[170]

On November 2, Grant told Halleck of his plan to move four infantry divisions from Corinth and Bolivar, Tennessee, to Grand Junction. From there he would move south, on Holly Springs and Grenada. General James B. McPherson would command one wing of the army and General Charles Hamilton the other.[171] Halleck approved the plan on November 3. Grant's force numbered over thirty thousand at first. Halleck promised him twenty thousand more, as well as support from Memphis, Helena, Arkansas and New Orleans. From Memphis, as the campaign unfolded, General W.T. Sherman would advance from Memphis down the line of the Mississippi & Tennessee Railroad to join forces with Grant south of Holly Springs, near Oxford. From Helena, Union cavalry would cross the river at Friar's Point to get in the Confederates' left rear.[172] Grant would be cautious, but he anticipated little resistance in North Mississippi. He told Sherman, "The enemy at Holly Springs is now estimated at 30,000 men, in rather a disorganized condition."[173] He assured Halleck that "I have not the slightest apprehension of a reverse from present appearances."[174]

Nevertheless, Grant moved cautiously. He had been surprised and nearly defeated at Shiloh just eight months earlier, when he failed to realize the Confederates had concentrated at Corinth. But he had other worries and constraints as well. The command situation in Memphis—in

Grant's own department—was uncertain and frustrating. General John A. McClernand, a political friend of the president, with ties to the governor of Illinois and to the secretary of war, wanted to recruit and lead a force downriver, independent of Grant's control. Grant wanted support from Memphis, but he wanted it from Sherman, not McClernand. It was a vexing distraction.

Grant also worried about his line of supply. The Civil War has often been called the "first railroad war," for good reason. By the time Grant planned his campaign, railroads had already played a spectacular role in the war. In July 1861, General Thomas J. Jackson had used the Manassas Gap Railroad to get his brigade to Manassas in time for the war's first battle, where he became "Stonewall" Jackson. On April 12, 1862, the Great Locomotive Chase highlighted the strategic importance of the Western & Atlantic Railroad between Atlanta and Chattanooga. On July 23, 1862, the Mobile & Ohio Railroad began carrying Bragg's Army of Tennessee from Tupelo to Mobile, the first leg of an incredible logistical feat that brought the army to Chattanooga. From there, Bragg launched his campaign into Kentucky. But thus far, no railroad had been placed in the position the Mississippi Central now found itself: the primary line of supply for an army advancing into enemy territory.

Given these worries, Grant was careful to find out where the Confederates were, and in what strength. As he moved south from Grand Junction, he put "one of the best cavalry officers I ever saw," Colonel Albert Lee, of the 7th Kansas Cavalry, in command of a large reconnaissance force and vanguard.[175]

Van Dorn lacked the strength to stop the Union advance. He could do little more than supply Pemberton with accurate information. He had to be wary, not least of the Federal force in Helena. If Union cavalry were to cross the river to gain his rear, he could be cut off from the crossings of the Tallahatchie River or, farther south, the Yalobusha. Colonel William H. Jackson, his cavalry commander, would have to be vigilant.

On November 3, Pemberton came to Holly Springs to review Van Dorn's army. Mary Ann Webster Loughborough was a guest. She wrote that the men "presented a fine appearance, most of them were newly uniformed…Van Dorn galloped up and down the line on a fleet, beautiful black horse…a proud, youthful head, surrounded by curls… the finest horseman in the army." Mrs. Carrington Mason, who lived in Holly Springs, had a different memory: "It was a sorry sight. Many of our men were bare headed and all were shabby, [but] I don't remember ever to have seen a despondent Confederate soldier."[176]

There was a ball that evening for the generals and their staffs. Mrs. Loughborough was enjoying a pleasant evening when suddenly, "in the midst of a conversation, an officer told me that the Federal forces were advancing on Holly Springs and that probably the Confederate forces would evacuate the area in a day or two…there is no telling where I will be when I write next."[177]

By November 10, the main body of Van Dorn's army had crossed the Tallahatchie, though a small detachment remained at Holly Springs.[178] Lee's force pushed them out on the thirteenth. "I have just entered this city [Holly Springs] and my pickets are polluting the 'sacred soil' some 2 miles below it." Lee pushed on two miles farther that same day, reporting, curiously, that "Van Dorn is not in arrest." He encountered stiff resistance from Jackson's cavalry, with artillery support. He warned that without reinforcements, he could not hold Holly Springs.[179]

Nevertheless, he sensed a chance to overtake and overwhelm Van Dorn's army between the Tallahatchie and the Yalobusha.[180] He still had between five and six hundred wagons with his army and was drawing half of his forage from the country. Halleck told him to draw more from the country. When Grant had asked him what he should do with "negroes coming in by wagon loads," Halleck told him to put them to work and, "so far as possible, subsist them and your army on the rebel inhabitants of Mississippi."[181]

But Grant believed that to attack Van Dorn and advance on Grenada, which he hoped to reach by January 1, he needed more logistical support than he had; he wanted to make full use of the railroad to establish a forward base of supply to support the operation he envisioned. He had the troops. Halleck had assured him on November 11, in reference to the rumors Grant had heard about McClernand's expedition, "You have command of all troops sent to your department, and have permission to fight the enemy where you please."[182]

Sherman would start down from Memphis on November 26 to join Grant south of Holly Springs. Grant wanted Sherman, McPherson and Hamilton to meet south of Holly Springs. On the twenty-ninth, Hamilton's infantry, following Lee's cavalry, closed in on Holly Springs. They pushed Jackson's cavalry south toward Lumpkin's Mill and on to within a few miles of the Tallahatchie. [183]

Mrs. Mason described the Federal army marching into Holly Springs: "First would pass by the regimental band…then, marching four abreast, in handsome new uniforms, came the infantry; and as the music of one regiment died away, the next could be heard in the distance. And so, on and on, for three days…a great blue monster…the wagon train was five days long."[184]

Grant arrived soon after Hamilton's infantry and established headquarters at Holly Springs later in the day. Soon, his wife, son and his wife's slave took up residence at Walter Place, the home of one of the founding fathers of the Mississippi Central and said to be the last great mansion built in the South before the war.[185]

Quartermaster Lieutenant Colonel C.A. Reynolds also established his headquarters there, with orders "to make Holly Springs for the present your main depot for supplies and get forward there all the supplies of every kind needed, and issue from there as required."[186] Union quartermasters and commissary officers commandeered buildings in town for storage space.

By that time, Van Dorn doubted he could hold anything north of Grenada: "We must have more troops," he wrote to Pemberton.[187] Van Dorn had moved his headquarters to Abbeville, covering the Tallahatchie bridge and the crossing at Rocky Ford, between New Albany and Abbeville.[188]

Grant's plan was now in motion. It "began working when the Helena expedition forced rebel commanders to look southwest." Grant intended Brigadier General Alvin Hovey's expedition as both a diversion and a real threat. But it was also a real threat to Confederate lines of communication and retreat toward Grenada.[189]

Van Dorn could only give ground. Something close to despair began to set in, from the men in Van Dorn's army to Pemberton's headquarters in Jackson. From Abbeville, Van Dorn reported that Sherman's column, whose strength he did not know, was near Chulahoma, about twenty miles southwest of Holly Springs. Van Dorn knew he could not hold Oxford. At the same time, Pemberton appealed to General Bragg for help: Sherman's army was on the move to join Grant, Grant would soon be over the Tallahatchie and an assault on Vicksburg seemed imminent. "You see my situation," he concluded. "It is for you to decide how far you can help me. I am now [November 30] moving my baggage to Yalabusha [*sic*]."[190] He conveyed his news to Jefferson Davis as well: "I am endeavoring to place myself behind the Yalabusha [*sic*] River, but am strongly threatened both in front and rear. Am now at Oxford, but shall move to-morrow morning."[191] John Milton Hubbard, a trooper in the 7th Tennessee Cavalry, was just as full of foreboding: "Our prospects were getting worse. North Mississippi was in the hands of the Federals and nothing seemed more probable or possible than we should be driven further toward the Gulf."[192]

By the night of November 29, Grant's advance was several miles south of Holly Springs. Abbeville, where the railroad crossed the Tallahatchie, lay just ahead. Private Banks, Van Dorn's critic in the 43rd Mississippi, thought that Van Dorn might fight on the Tallahatchie—unless he was flanked. In that case, "Pemberton will show his skill at that masterly mode of defense—a skedaddle."[193] Van Dorn could not fight on the Tallahatchie. The force in his front was too great, and he was worried about the Union cavalry off to the southwest.

On December 1, Grant reported, "Our cavalry are now crossing Tallahatchie…The rebels are evidently retreating. If so, I will follow to Oxford. Our troops will be in Abbeville to-morrow…Sherman is up and will cross the Tallahatchie at Wyatt." But on the night of December 2, General Hovey, commanding the Helena cavalry expedition threatening Van Dorn's line of retreat to Grenada, decided to turn west and return to Helena.[194] One detachment of his force, under General Cadwallader Washburn, had been skirmishing around Oakland, more or less continuously with Colonel John S. Griffith's brigade of Texas cavalry. Oakland was on the Mississippi & Tennessee Railroad, about twenty miles north of Grenada. It was also an important road junction. Two roads intersected at Oakland. One ran east to Coffeeville, about twenty miles away, on the Mississippi Central Railroad, and west to Friars Point and the crossing to Helena. The other road came down from the north, crossing the Tallahatchie forty miles west of Abbeville and going on to Grenada. Van Dorn and Griffith knew that a Union force at Oakland was a threat to Coffeeville, if they made a stand there, and to their line of retreat to Grenada. Oakland had to be held. Van Dorn, therefore, "ordered Griffith's cavalry to pounce."[195] Perhaps unaware that Hovey's force was now withdrawing, Griffith moved to Oakland where he clashed with Washburn's detachment on December 3. Griffith reported that as he drew near to the Federals, just north of town, a battery of Washburn's artillery opened fire on him, "pouring in grape and canister at a fearful rate and with a rapidity that exceeded anything I ever saw before." Undaunted, Griffith charged the battery (actually a section of two guns) and took it. When more Union artillery opened fire on his flank, Griffith fell back to town, bringing one of the two captured guns with him. His

Colonel John Summerfield Griffith, 1829–1901. Griffith proposed the Holly Springs raid to General Pemberton. Ill health led to his resignation in 1863, but he was commissioned brigadier general of Texas state troops in 1864. *Courtesy of John Anderson, Preservation Officer, Archives and Information Services Division, Texas State Library & Archives Commission.*

men did well off the battlefield, he reported, picking up "six shooters, coats, blankets, hats &c."[196] Griffith assured Van Dorn that he would "get after and harass them...I can and will keep them back from Oakland."[197] The Union cavalry continued its withdrawal toward Helena, while Van Dorn's army continued its withdrawal toward Coffeeville.

On December 4–5, Union troops were on the square in Oxford. Grant asked Halleck, "How far south would you like me to go?"[198] (Halleck had told him on November 25, "Do not go too far.")

The Confederate army was miserable: cold, wet, hungry and still falling back. Thomas Weir, of the 4th Mississippi, wrote on December 4: "At 3 p.m. we close in and start for Coffeeville. It rains all day and night

Grant on the square at Oxford, Mississippi. The tents are of an Illinois regiment. Grant was in Oxford at the time of the raid. Federal troops burned the courthouse in 1864. *From* The Photographic History of the Civil War in Ten Volumes, *ed. Francis Trevelyan Miller, vol. 2.*

but we press through the mud, which in many places is over our boot tops…we are wet to the skin. We bivouac three miles from town on the railroad in the rain…no sleep, no provisions."[199]

Grant was unable to take advantage of the Confederates' plight. On December 5, Lovell's infantry stopped Colonel T. Lyle Dickey's 3,500 cavalry at Coffeeville, in an engagement that claimed nearly 100 casualties and forced the Federals to fall back to Water Valley. Van Dorn reported to Pemberton, "Night put a stop to pursuit. He [Grant] will be careful how he comes up again."[200] Dickey's losses were 10 killed, 63 wounded and 41 missing.[201]

The fights at Oakland and Coffeeville bought Van Dorn time and leeway to get his army over the Yalobusha and behind what is called the Yalobusha Line—earthworks in varying stages of preparation, stretching east to Columbus, Mississippi. They were mostly unmanned and unfinished, except at Columbus and Grenada where they were very strong. There were eight solid earthwork forts at Grenada, two or three of which can still be seen.[202]

Grant, moreover, was still concerned with Memphis and what might be brewing there between McClernand and his cronies in Springfield and Washington. Halleck's assurances to Grant were unclear and sometimes close to contradictory. On December 4, Grant made a suggestion that could reconfigure the campaign: "I will cut the Mobile road south of Tupelo. Would it not be well to hold the enemy south of [the] Yalabusha [*sic*] and move a force from Memphis [under Sherman, who would return there] and Helena on Vicksburg? With my present force it would not be safe to go beyond Grenada and attempt to hold present lines of communication."[203]

On December 5, the day of the engagement at Coffeeville, Halleck told Grant, "I think you should not attempt to hold the country south of the Tallahatchie." "Your main object," he went on, "will be to hold the line from Memphis to Corinth with as small a force as possible, while the largest number possible is thrown upon Vicksburg with the gunboats." Then, on the 7th, Halleck told Grant to "move your troops as you may deem best."[204]

If there was going to be a downriver expedition, Grant wanted Sherman to lead it. He was willing to send Sherman back to Memphis to do so. "The second week of December found Grant engrossed in sending Sherman back to Memphis."[205] On December 9, he told Halleck: "Sherman has already gone [to Memphis]. The enterprise would be much safer in [his] charge."[206] Grant now proposed to cooperate with Sherman's downriver expedition by maintaining his presence and fronting the Confederates on the Yalobusha.

At this point, Grant decided to send a cavalry force east to cut the line of the Mobile & Ohio Railroad. Late on December 13, he ordered Colonel Dickey, with eight hundred picked men, to leave the main body and head east to strike the Mobile & Ohio Railroad between Okolona and Tupelo. The next morning, Dickey left Water Valley for Pontotoc, forty-three miles east. Even in the heavy rain and cold they moved fast, reaching Pontotoc on the fifteenth and going on from there to strike the railroad at Okolona. They burned bridges and depots and tore up tracks before turning back from Harrisburg, near Tupelo, on the morning of December 18.[207] Later that day, opportunity would almost literally stare Dickey in the face.

Meantime, another irritant distressed Grant—one so great that he fired off General Orders No. 11 to eradicate it. Perhaps he was feeling some of the same frustrations that had led Van Dorn to put Vicksburg under martial law back in July. Grant ordered the expulsion of all Jews from his department, alleging that they had violated "every regulation of trade established by the Treasury Department and also department orders." They were to be issued passes through and out of his lines and were to be gone within twenty-four hours.[208]

His most nagging concern was still supplies. By December 3, the Mississippi Central was running smoothly southward to Holly Springs. But the roads were muddy and near impassable south of there. When he established headquarters in Oxford, he ordered that railroad repairs be pushed as far as the Tallahatchie as fast as possible. He wrote to his sister on December 15: "I am extended now like a peninsula into an enemy's country and with a large army depending for their daily bread upon keeping open a line of railroad running one hundred and ninety miles through an enemy's country or, at least through territory occupied by a people terribly embittered and hostile to us."[209]

On the day he wrote, General Nathan Bedford Forrest crossed the Tennessee River at Clifton, Tennessee, aiming for Grant's line supply near Jackson, Tennessee, about seventy miles distant. Grant soon learned of Forrest's presence in West Tennessee and worried about it. He did not know, however, of an even greater threat to his railroad lifeline looming in North Mississippi.

Chapter 6

"Van Dorn, Than Whom No Braver Man Lives"

The news from Mississippi reaching the War Department in Richmond had been bad all through November and into December. Grant's advance appeared irresistible. Still, President Davis knew that Vicksburg's defenses were far stronger now than in the summer. Furthermore, Grant's army was 150 miles away from Vicksburg and halted, at least temporarily, in front of the strong Confederate position at Grenada. The Confederate command structure in the west left something to be desired, even if there was nothing in it remotely comparable to the McClernand snafu in Grant's Department of the Tennessee. What it lacked was unified command and a way of coordinating the movements of Bragg's army in Tennessee and Pemberton's in Mississippi.

In late November, Davis made a bold and innovative attempt to achieve unified command in the west. He created what would today be called a theater command for the Confederacy's third-ranking full general, Joseph E. Johnston. Johnston would have no field command but did have authority, at least in the president's eyes, to coordinate the movements of the two field armies in what was now the Department of the West. Johnston came to believe that he had, in fact, no authority over these armies, and in the end, Davis's plans came to naught. Johnston certainly had no authority beyond the Mississippi into Arkansas, where Holmes stood aloof. Pemberton raised the issue of Arkansas in an early report to Johnston, noting that while the Federals could bring troops over the river, he could not.[210]

On December 9, Mississippi Senator James Phelan made the same point in his letter to Jefferson Davis. But he went much further than that. Coming from one of Davis's strongest supporters,[211] Phelan's letter was worse than disheartening. It was devastating, even doomsaying. Phelan reported that the situation was dire, a complete shambles, with the army in a "most deplorable state as to its morale and organization." The fact that Union cavalry had crossed the river from Arkansas to threaten the army's flank appalled Phelan. Worse, it was a staggering blow to Pemberton's reputation. But worst of all was that

> *few even know that General Pemberton is at the head of the army...it is yet called "Van Dorn's army," and the universal opprobrium which covers that officer and the "lower than the lowest deep" to which he has fallen...you cannot be aware of. He may be but an illustration of the proverb "Give a dog a bad name," but so it is...he is regarded as the sower of all our woes...the atmosphere is dense with horrid narratives of his negligence, whoring, and drunkenness, for the truth of which I cannot vouch, but it is so fastened in the public belief that as acquittal by a court martial of angels would not relieve him of the charge.*[212]

Finished with Van Dorn, Phelan described a political and military situation so desperate that only Davis could save it. "Plant your own foot upon our soil, unfurl your banner at the head of the army...If ever your presence was needed...this is the hour. It is not a point to be argued."[213]

President Davis could not take the field in Mississippi, but he did travel west to confer with Johnston, Bragg and Pemberton. He left Richmond perhaps as early as December 10 and was gone from the capital for twenty-seven days.[214]

Van Dorn was the subject of a second letter in early December, this one from a friend and addressed to Pemberton. The letter was from John S. Griffith, the hard-fighting Texas colonel whose brigade had crossed swords with the Federal cavalry at Oakland on December 3. Griffith was a Marylander but now hailed from Kaufman City, Texas.[215] He and his men admired Van Dorn, perhaps because of his earlier service in their state. There had been some ill will when Van Dorn dismounted some of the regiments before Corinth, but he had procured new mounts from the Trans-Mississippi and so returned to their good graces.[216]

The letter bore Griffith's signature and those of his regimental commanders. Supporting signees were Lieutenant Colonel E.R. Hawkins and Major J.H. Brooks of the 1st Texas Legion, Lieutenant Colonel J.S. Boggess of the 3rd Texas Cavalry, Lieutenant Colonel D.W. Jones of the 9th Texas Cavalry and Captain Jack Wharton of the 6th Texas Cavalry. Griffith began tactfully, begging leave,

> *modestly to suggest the propriety of a cavalry expedition into the enemy's rear…the best employment in which the cavalry under your command, can be engaged…if you will fit up a cavalry expedition comprising three or four thousand men, and give us Major General Earl Van Dorn, than whom no braver man lives, we will penetrate the rear of the enemy, capture Holly Springs, Memphis and other points, and perhaps, force him…to retreat from Coffeeville; if not we can certainly force more of the enemy to remain in the rear, to protect their supplies, than the cavalry could whip if we remained at the front.*[217]

Pemberton replied immediately to arrange a meeting with Griffith but was in Vicksburg until December 12. By the time Pemberton reached Grenada, he was aware that Forrest had crossed the Tennessee River to strike at Grant's supply line in West Tennessee. A simultaneous attack on Grant's line of supply in North Mississippi might reap rich benefits. Pemberton was willing to try. But Griffith's request that Van Dorn, specifically, lead the raid in North Mississippi was potentially awkward.[218] Van Dorn would have to step down to a small cavalry command, and the present cavalry commander, Colonel William Jackson, would serve under Van Dorn. Eight months earlier, when Van Dorn had an infantry command under Beauregard at the siege of Corinth, he had taken personal offense at a brother officer's mere suggestion that he consider leading a cavalry raid behind Federal lines. General St. John Richardson Liddell, whose suggestion it was, mentioned the incident to General William Hardee. Hardee laughed and said, "It was asking too much of Van Dorn to give up a corps of infantry for a cavalry command."[219]

It may have been asking too much in April, but it was not in December. When Pemberton authorized Griffith's proposal, Van Dorn seized the opportunity. His orders were clear, but they left much to his discretion. He was to "swing around Grant's left flank, strike the big enemy supply depot at Holly Springs, and wreak havoc on the Mississippi Central & Memphis & Charleston Railroads."[220] He would take Griffith's brigade and those of Colonel W.H. Jackson and Colonel Robert "Black Bob" McCulloch, numbering in all perhaps 3,500 men.[221]

Van Dorn's Command[222]

Escort—1ˢᵗ Confederate Regular Cavalry, Co. A	Capt. John Bradley
Jackson's Brigade (approx. 1,200 men)	**Col. William H. Jackson**
3ʳᵈ Tennessee Cavalry	Lt. Col. Robert Balch
6ᵗʰ Tennessee Cavalry	Col. James T. Wheeler
7ᵗʰ Tennessee Cavalry	Col. William H. Jackson
McCulloch's Brigade (approx. 800 men)	**Col. Robert McCulloch**
1ˢᵗ Mississippi Cavalry	Col. Richard A. Pinson
2ⁿᵈ Missouri Cavalry	Col. Robert McCulloch
3ʳᵈ Arkansas Cavalry—Cos. A, B, I and K	Col. Samuel G. Earle
Griffith's Texas Brigade	**Col. John S. Griffith**
3ʳᵈ Texas Cavalry	Lt. Col. Jiles S. Boggess Jr.
Willis's Texas Battalion	Capt. Thomas M. Harwood
6ᵗʰ Texas Cavalry	Capt. Jack Wharton
9ᵗʰ Texas Cavalry	Lt. Col. Dudley W. Jones
1ˢᵗ Texas Legion	Col. Edwin R. Hawkins

The operation would be extremely difficult and dangerous. Success would depend on a combination of factors, all resting squarely on Van Dorn's shoulders. His resolve, boldness and steadiness (i.e., leadership) were crucial. Cavalry operations behind enemy lines require a special kind of daring and audacity. Van Dorn had it. Four months earlier, in the mournful and angry retreat from the Battle of Corinth, Van Dorn had rashly proposed attacking again. Those around him were naturally aghast. Maury wrote that a friend told Van Dorn, "You are the only man I ever saw who loves danger for its own sake…You cannot adequately estimate the obstacles in your way." Van Dorn immediately abandoned his foolish proposal, in effect apologizing for even thinking of endangering the army "through my personal peculiarities."[223] Now, in December, Van Dorn's personality had not changed, but the opportunity had. It now suited his personality. Griffith knew his man.

Earl Van Dorn, 1820–1863. "Van Dorn had one of those antebellum faces of tumult and recklessness, which truly expressed his spirit."— Clifford Dowdey, 1946. *From* The Photographic History of the Civil War in Ten Volumes, *ed. Francis Trevelyan Miller, vol. 2.*

Van Dorn looked the part, as well. He was described at the time as "about 40 years of age [he was forty-two], small of stature, dark skinned, dark beard, bright, keen black eyes, clean cut and well defined features, straight as an Indian, sitting his horse like a knight and looking every inch a soldier."[224]

From the very beginning, Van Dorn shrouded the operation in secrecy. "We mounted without knowing where we were going," wrote W.L. Stevenson, of the 3rd Texas.[225] He kept the destination from his men for as long as possible. Once McCulloch's and Jackson's brigades left their camps to join Griffith's brigade behind Grenada, most of the men guessed that their mission was to protect the line of the Mobile & Ohio, farther east.

Riding east, as far as Houston and/or Pontotoc, would cloak the mission in deception; they were riding east, but their target was the Mississippi Central, not the Mobile & Ohio. Once they had turned north, any Federals they encountered must be made to think that Van Dorn was headed farther north to Tennessee to meet Forrest. But his ultimate destination lay to the west, not the north. Nowhere along his route could he become engaged with any Federals; he had to move fast and linger nowhere. He would bring no artillery or wagons. Pack mules bore vats of turpentine and boxes of matches. Finally, Van Dorn had to hope that in addition to leadership, secrecy, deception and speed, luck would favor the bold.

Van Dorn's men did not know their destination, but they did see that the long and dispiriting retreat was over. Through weeks of cold, rain and mud, they had become dispirited, but they had not lost their resolve. Alexander Chadwell, of Company E in McCulloch's 2nd Missouri Cavalry, was glad to be riding toward Missouri and home, to lift the heel of Federal tyranny from his family and state.[226]

On December 15, Chadwell's regiment moved up to within four miles of Grenada, stopping south of town to cook rations. "We got to cooking about 10 o'clock in the night and cooked up about two days rations, laid down and slept until 4 o'clock when we saddled up and started back to Grenada."[227] They arrived at Streathan's Plantation (now the Grenada Municipal Airport) in Grenada just after daylight and rested

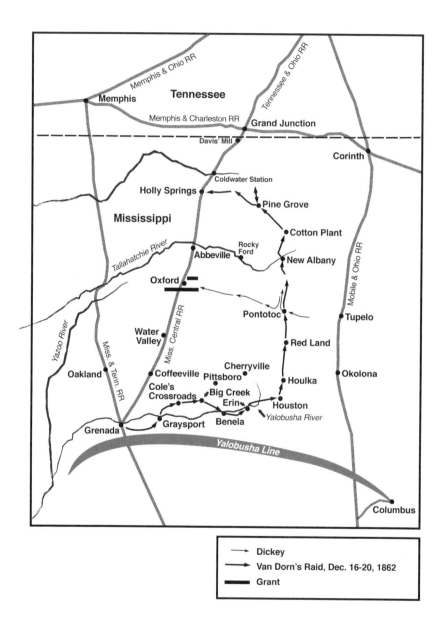

Van Dorn rides north from Grenada. *By Marshall Hudson.*

briefly. They left before dawn on Tuesday, December 16, headed for Graysport, crossed the river and continued on the "Houston Road."[228]

The Confederates pushed on throughout the day, and then in darkness until about midnight, when Van Dorn permitted a halt of four hours. They had covered forty-five miles since daybreak.[229] It had been a tiring day, but morale and anticipation were high.

The men still did not know their destination. Riding east might have fueled speculation that they were bound for the Mobile & Ohio; the depots and trackside corncribs at Okolona were just twenty miles northeast. But then Van Dorn turned due north. His men did not halt on the night of the seventeenth until they were thirteen miles beyond Houston.

It is difficult to trace Van Dorn's route to Holly Springs with certainty. For example, in his study of the raid, Tom Parson has Van Dorn passing south of Pittsborough to Houston. Several Confederate accounts mention passing through Houston. Other historians do not believe they went to Houston. Local historians in Houston believe that Van Dorn came no closer than Cherry Hill, west of Houston. However they went, it was a long and tiring ride in mostly bad weather. The extent to which young troopers, most of whom were not Mississippians, may have known where they were on the map is open to question. They certainly camped north of Houston on the night of the seventeenth, passed through Pontotoc and camped just north of New Albany on the night of the eighteenth.

They moved out again at sunrise on December 18, headed north (but still within reach of the Mobile & Ohio Railroad). This was a crucial day, when the expedition had a close brush with ruin. The day began promisingly enough with their arrival at Pontotoc, where they were greeted with an enthusiastic welcome. One trooper recalled "extravagant demonstrations of joy."[230] Alexander Chadwell wrote that as they "passed through Pontotoc, the citizens seemed very glad to see us, particularly the ladies who waved their handkerchiefs and greeted us with smiles."[231] James C. Bates, a sergeant in the 9th Texas, had never seen "such wild demonstrations of joy as were exhibited by the ladies of Pontotoc and in fact of every little town that we passed through…soldiers receiving meat and bread, milk &c."[232] Van Dorn, however, did not linger. His destination that day was New Albany, twenty miles farther on.

It was good that he did not linger. His was not the only cavalry force at, or very near, Pontotoc that day. Colonel Dickey's force, returning from its raid on the Mobile & Ohio, had halted six miles east of Pontotoc but was now moving due west for Oxford. Van Dorn's route north cut squarely across Dickey's route west. Sylvanus Cadwallader, a correspondent for the *Chicago Times*, who was with Dickey, wrote, "We could plainly see Van Dorn's men marching along the road, crossing our line of retreat." Had there been a clash, the Federals would likely have been overwhelmed. But according to Cadwallader, Dickey believed that the Confederates' objective was to find him. Cadwallader went on: "Dickey seemed to think that Van Dorn would certainly pursue him and that if he could manage to escape…it would cover him with glory…[but Van Dorn] was after larger game…he did not so much as halt his column when Dickey appeared in his rear."[233]

Van Dorn refused to be diverted. As the Confederates continued north, Dickey shadowed them for a few miles, staying off to the west. There may have been a small clash a few miles north of Pontotoc, but Dickey soon turned away, headed for Oxford. Van Dorn continued north toward the Tallahatchie at New Albany. Dickey ordered couriers, with an escort, to ride ahead to tell Grant, who was then at Oxford, that a large body of Confederate cavalry was moving north from Pontotoc. But when Dickey made camp that night, he was shocked to discover that "the escort and couriers by a fatal misapprehension of my orders had not left the column." It is difficult to see how his orders could have been misunderstood, or, as he went on to explain, how the next set of couriers "lost their way in the Yockna [*sic*] Bottom, and traveling at night found themselves farther from Oxford than when they left camp, and did not arrive until this morning."[234]

Van Dorn camped that night, December 18, on the north bank of the Tallahatchie, near New Albany, in a hard rain. Some of the camps flooded. They were probably glad to get an early start on the morning of the nineteenth. Meanwhile, Dickey's news—that a large force of Confederate cavalry was moving north from Pontotoc—reached Grant sometime on the afternoon of the nineteenth. The news was startling and, for the moment, correct. Grant reacted to the news with a flurry of orders to Hamilton, McPherson, Brigadier General Grenville Dodge (near Corinth), Colonel J.K. Mizner (at Water Valley) and, as a precaution, to commanders along the line of the Mississippi Central. But by that evening, the news was no longer correct. Unknown to Grant, Van Dorn was now headed west, not north.

For most of the day, the nineteenth, Van Dorn was on the Ripley Road, headed north. But at Cotton Plant, he took a road to the northwest. That road forked at Pine Grove, with one branch leading north to Spring Hill, Grand Junction and Bolivar and the other west to Holly Springs. Van Dorn took the road to Bolivar. Then, probably under cover of darkness, he led his men back to Pine Grove to take the Holly Springs Road.[235]

Grant's first dispatches, therefore, were wide of the mark. To begin with, Grant assumed that the cavalry was Colonel William Jackson's. Thus, Hamilton was "to rescue Colonel Dickey." McPherson was to halt his advance: "We must be ready for any move." Colonel Mizner, commanding a brigade of cavalry at Water Valley, was to get on "Jackson's" trail and "follow him until he is caught or dispersed. Jackson must be prevented from getting to the railroad in our rear." He ordered Mizner to get to Rocky Ford on the Tallahatchie, between Abbeville and New Albany. Then, as a precaution, he telegraphed the garrisons at Bolivar, La Grange, Grand Junction, Davis' Mills and Holly Springs: "Keep a sharp lookout and defend the road, if attacked, at all hazards." Most important, as it turned out, was the message to Colonel Murphy at Holly Springs. Grant warned Murphy that "Jackson" was headed for the Tallahatchie, to cross at Rocky Ford. He ordered: "Send out all the cavalry you can to watch their movements." Murphy responded that his cavalry was on the move but asked, "Where is Rocky Ford that you speak of?" Grant explained that it was twenty miles from Abbeville on the Tallahatchie, adding, "In the morning will be early enough for your cavalry to start."[236]

MURPHY'S COMMAND[237]

2nd Illinois Cavalry—Cos. C, F, G, H, I and K	Lt. Col. Quincy McNeil
29th Illinois Infantry—Cos. A, B, C, E, F, G, H and I	Maj. John A. Callicott
62nd Illinois Infantry (approx. 200 men)	Maj. Stephen M. Meeker
101st Illinois Infantry	Col. Charles H. Fox

Both Mizner and, more importantly, Murphy let Grant down on the night of December 19. Writing in the aftermath of the raid, Major John J. Mudd, of the 2nd Illinois Cavalry, claimed that his regiment was given no warning whatsoever: "This disaster is another added to the long list occasioned by the drunkenness or inefficiency of commanding officers." Murphy's officers were for the most part not in their camps at all but were "quietly sleeping at the houses of rebel citizens."[238]

There were no tents, and little sleep, for Van Dorn's men. They rode in cold December darkness the rest of the way. No one suspected their presence, but the men now knew where they were going. As they moved west through the darkness, Van Dorn sent troopers familiar with Holly Springs ahead to reconnoiter; some may have put on civilian clothes and risked going in as spies. There are stories of knowing civilians organizing Christmas parties for Federal officers as distractions. As Van Dorn continued, the Holly Springs Road would, from time to time, divide into parallel roads; Van Dorn divided his command whenever that happened. The roads, and Van Dorn's command, came together finally on the Salem Road (today's Higdon Road), east of a prominent rise just outside of Holly Springs. It must have been an hour or two before first light. By then, Van Dorn had made his plans. He knew Holly Springs well. He also knew that the garrison was not alert, and he planned as if he knew what its positions were. The 101st Illinois infantry was in camps along the Mississippi Central tracks, mostly at the depot but both north and south of it as well. The 29th and 62nd Illinois Regiments were in and around the square. Depot Street (today's Van Dorn Avenue) ran from the depot to the square. North of the square, at the town's fairgrounds, was the camp of the 2nd Illinois Cavalry.

Van Dorn's plan was shrewd. Griffith's brigade would ride over and through the 101st Illinois camps at the depot and then thunder down Depot Street to the square. McCulloch's brigade would cross the railroad north of the depot; the 1st Mississippi Cavalry would cross the tracks and then veer toward the fairgrounds, while McCulloch's 2nd Missouri and 3rd Arkansas, dismounted, would "mop up" the shattered 101st Illinois around the depot. Once Griffith had secured the square, he would support the 1st Mississippi at the fairgrounds and guard the roads coming into Holly Springs from the south. Jackson's brigade would ride northward, along the railroad, toward the headwaters of the Coldwater to block access to Holly Springs from the north.[239]

At this point, some men had to be detailed to see that the mules—the bearers of turpentine and matches—were brought up as soon as the cavalry charged. Or it may be that the turpentine went into canteens. In any event, no braying mules could sound the alarm now.

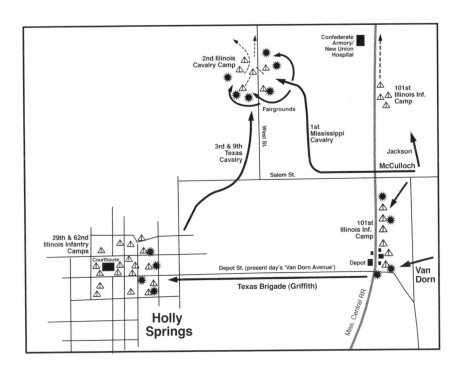

Over the next rise—Van Dorn's attack on Holly Springs. *By Marshall Hudson.*

Once the plan was set, the last perilous step was to silence the picket posts, muffling them without firing a shot. Lieutenants Hyams and Day led small detachments forward. Murphy's command was probably past saving by that time, but no shots were fired.[240] Holly Springs—and Grant's stores—lay just over the next rise.

Chadwell wrote: "Dismounted [we] held our horses in column until just before daylight when we mounted and moved on silently and stealthily, orders having been given for keeping the strictest silence."[241]

Griffith's vision was about to be realized. They were on the verge of crippling a mighty army. Leadership, secrecy, deception, speed and luck had brought them to the edge of Holly Springs. They waited now for first light and Van Dorn's order to charge. The men at the head of the columns looked toward Van Dorn. W.R. Stevenson, of the 3rd Texas, saw him: "On a little rise, seated on his fine black mare, holding his hat above his head, I thought him as fine a figure as I had ever seen."[242] Colonel

Van Dorn's command waited on this side of the rise in the background before Van Dorn pointed his sword, an unspoken order to charge. *Photograph by Garrie Colhoun.*

82

"Van Dorn, Than Whom No Braver Man Lives"

Griffith wrote later, "I felt as if I could charge hell and capture the devil, if the Almighty had commanded me to do so."[243] Colonel Brown described the last few hundred yards of their ride from Grenada:

> *The white tents of the camp were in full view. On a slight eminence near the roadside…were three or four horsemen; in passing them General Van Dorn was recognized…with a tremendous cheer which he gracefully acknowledged and pointed to the enemy with his sword. The effect of the silent order was electrical…in another moment we struck the enemy like a thunderbolt.*[244]

Chapter 7

Van Dorn on the Square in Holly Springs

I n Holly Springs, Mrs. Mason had laid a fire before going to bed. She recalled later: "On the morning of December 20 as I lay in bed I heard a sound which I thought was the singing of the wood fire, but on going near it I found that the sound came from a distance. Raising the window I cried out 'Oh it is the Rebel yell.'"[245]

The sound was terrifying and fast moving. Trooper Hubbard, in the 7th Tennessee, wrote that his column was "moving so rapidly that we made the last mile or two at about full speed. When we did reach the town the horses were hot and smoking."[246]

The sleeping soldiers of the 101st Illinois awoke to a nightmare of havoc and confusion. The cavalry rode right through their camps, and behind them came McCulloch's dismounted Missouri and Arkansas troopers. Men surrendered by the score, and Confederates herded hundreds of prisoners together, left them under guard and pushed onto the square. The surprise had been all that Van Dorn had hoped for. Chadwell wrote, "Going in from the east side by the depot we made no halt until we reached the public square…from almost every house might be seen the frightened Yankees as they rushed into the streets to make their escape."[247]

Colonel Murphy reported that he was captured at the depot. Other reports had him caught in his nightshirt at his residence, the Hugh Craft

Van Dorn on the Square in Holly Springs

Mississippi Central depot, 1862. An artist for *Harper's Weekly*, A. Simplot, made this sketch shortly before the raid. The building in the left rear is still standing. *From a copy in the author's collection.*

Mississippi Central depot, 2011. The same area today, with the former Illinois Central passenger station and antebellum freight house. *Photograph by Garrie Colhoun.*

house. Except for six companies of the 101st Illinois, which were camped north of the depot near a trestle over the Coldwater River, very few of Murphy's men escaped. The six companies reached the camps of the 90th Illinois Volunteers ("the Chicago Irish Legion") at the headwaters of the Coldwater.[248]

Total confusion reigned in the center of town. Mrs. Mason saw "citizens, negroes, Yankees, and Rebels…squads of Federal prisoners were being brought in faster than they could be paroled, and there were not Confederates enough to guard them."[249]

Mrs. Mason was an astute observer. Van Dorn could neither guard nor bring out prisoners. Guarding them would slow the work of destruction; bringing them out would imperil the raiders' escape. The prisoners had to be paroled (i.e., released on condition that they not serve again until notified of a proper exchange of paroled prisoners). Most prisoners were paroled on the spot or soon after. The irregularity was essential to Van Dorn but damning to Murphy. He was later accused of aiding and abetting the enemy in an all too ready willingness to accept parole.[250]

Citizens thronged the square. A woman told Private Carr of the 9th Texas where to find one Union officer she had seen in hiding. Carr followed her directions and demanded his surrender. The officer, a colonel, refused at first to surrender to a lesser rank. Carr told him that he, too, was a colonel and had his prisoner.[251]

Courthouse Square, 1862. Simplot's sketch of the square at Holly Springs in 1862. *From a copy in the author's collection.*

Van Dorn on the Square in Holly Springs

The square in June 2011. *Photograph by Garrie Colhoun.*

It was a different story at the fairgrounds, the camp of the 2nd Illinois Cavalry. The Illinois troopers were awake when Van Dorn charged into town, probably preparing to move out in the search for "Jackson" that Grant had ordered for that morning. The 1st Mississippi Cavalry came crashing headlong into them, but they did not panic or surrender. Their colonel, Quincy McNeil, was already in the saddle with one company. The Mississippians rode right over them, capturing McNeil, but his company commanders fought on without him. Confederates called it "a spirited defense" and a "sharp little fight." Colonel Brown saw one officer come "riding furiously at our line, and when ordered to surrender paid no attention to the summons except to draw his revolver and fire in our faces. His fire was returned and he fell mortally wounded."[252]

Texas trooper W.P. McMinn described a saber duel between a Colonel Montgomery and a Federal officer, "the first and only fight of this kind that I witnessed during the war. The Yankee made about two licks at Colonel Montgomery...[who] got one of his fingers nearly cut off...

When the Yankee officer saw that his men had not followed, he turned and ran. We went after them."[253]

J.G. Deupree, in the 1st Mississippi Cavalry, saw another furious saber duel in which a friend was "seriously cut in the forehead, and the blood gushed." But he recalled "pistols in the hands of Mississippians proved superior to sabers wielded by the hardy sons of Illinois."[254] Several companies of the Illinois cavalry fought their way out of the mêlée in the fairgrounds. Most rode north toward the Chicago Irish Legion's camp, but one company rode straight into town, right into the square. Lieutenant Chadwell wrote that "a squad of cavalry came dashing into the square but before they had time to form our boys gave them a volley which sent them dashing out again."[255] Those Federals who got out of town stayed out of town. Jackson's brigade, guarding the roads north of town, left them alone. When the destruction began in Holly Springs, Jackson pulled his men back into town.[256]

In all, the 2nd Illinois lost eight killed, thirty-nine wounded and about one hundred captured.[257] One Texas trooper in the 9th took eight prisoners himself in a stable while finding himself "a mule with a good saddle."[258]

The fight at the fairgrounds ended Union resistance. Murphy's command no longer existed. Van Dorn's task now was to destroy Grant's stores, and quickly. There was no alternative to destruction. Van Dorn had neither the "thousands of wagons"[259] nor the time to carry off the immense amount of stores Grant's quartermasters had accumulated. It would all have to be destroyed. But he allowed his men to keep what they could wear, carry or ride; his officers' challenge was to maintain reasonable discipline. The men had noticed right away that their prisoners "were a well dressed set."[260] Soon they began to see what was behind a well-fed, well-appointed army. As buildings were emptied and crates and barrels opened, it all began to dawn on Deupree and hundreds of others. "It was hard to believe that we were in possession of the greatest booty captured by any Confederate force thus far during the war. Everybody wanted to carry off something but it was difficult to make a selection."[261]

All manner of clothing, provisions, blankets, ammunition, medicine, carbines and six-shooters were there for the taking. It was not only army stores, but there were also the delicacies and novelties of the unlucky sutlers in Holly Springs. It was bad luck too for the cotton speculators in town. Deupree wrote, "The cotton speculators were in large force and had many hundred bales stored wherever they could find room." Soldiers burned the bales and emptied the speculators' pockets.[262]

Van Dorn's threadbare men seized any articles of clothing, including those of Union blue. "The boys said put on the blue clothes and when we get further down in Dixie we will change their color."[263] One trooper in the 7th Tennessee garnered "a string of hats as long as a plough line, wrapped about him and his horse.

The only civilian casualty. The grave of George R. Spradley, age ten, in Hill Crest Cemetery, Holly Springs. *Photograph by Garrie Colhoun.*

What with boots, hats, caps, shirts, and overcoats…we were transformed into Yankee cavalry."[264] "Six shooters and Sharp's rifles went almost begging."[265]

Griffith's men had ridden into Holly Springs on "Texas or Mexican saddles with roping horns. They left astride McClellan cavalry saddles. The Ninth's seventy-five [captured] cavalry horses were equipped with small black leather saddle bags, regulation saddle blankets, carbine buckets and pistol holsters, all the tack a cavalryman could desire."[266]

In short, Van Dorn's force rode away from Holly Springs as "the best equipped body of cavalry in the Confederate service."[267] But Van Dorn had not come to Holly Springs to outfit and equip three brigades of

Confederate cavalry and celebrate the victory. He had come to cripple an invading army by destroying its quartermaster and commissary stores, i.e., bushels of wheat, barrels of beef, pork, flour, hardtack, coffee, loaded wagons, well-equipped ambulances, arms and ammunition—the necessary provisions for invasion. Destroying them was Van Dorn's only purpose. As Grant soon learned, "They destroyed everything they could not carry away."[268] An unnamed writer for the *Missouri Democrat*, who may have been an eyewitness, wrote that the Confederates "came prepared for such business, as all their canteens were filled with turpentine which they poured…and then touched off."[269] They worked in three places: around the depot, at the former armory (now a military hospital set to receive patients) and on the square.

The depot, with its trackside buildings, shops and strings of boxcars loaded with arms and ammunition, rations and clothing, showed how well Quartermaster C.M. Reynolds had followed his orders: "Make Holly Springs…your main depot…Forward there all the supplies of every kind."[270] "Standing on the track near the depot was a long string of boxcars loaded with rations and clothing for the army at the front, only waiting to get up steam enough to pull out. This was burned as it stood, and the engine was crippled."[271]

Flames engulfed the area. Only one building survived, the brick freight house that still stands beside the Illinois Central station today, 149 years later. Fire also claimed the old Jones-McElwaine Iron Foundry, later the armory. It was now fitted out as a well-equipped military hospital about to receive patients from the General Hospital on the square. Union surgeon Horace Wirtz called it "one of the most completely furnished and extensive hospitals in the army," with two thousand beds. Mrs. Anna Hillyer, whose husband was a colonel in the 13th Army Corps Provost Office, had visited the building the day before. "The arrangements were all complete," she wrote: fifteen hundred beds "nicely made," surgical apparatus on hand, boxes of bedding and clothing, kitchens complete and even "gymnastics," i.e., exercise facilities. It suggests that Grant envisioned a major battle.[272] When Wirtz saw smoke rising from the depot, he rushed to "the rebel general" to plead for his hospital. He assured him that the building would be protected and a guard posted to ensure it.

Wirtz soon learned, however, that the hospital had burned to the ground. Even worse, the destruction on the square, now underway, had claimed the old hospital. He charged that its patients had been roughly roused and marched out.[273] Citizens took in a few of these patients, Mrs. Hillyer wrote. One lady took in twenty soldiers and tended them in her parlor.[274]

The square, and the adjacent buildings, presented a difficult problem for the Confederates, with no good outcome possible for Holly Springs. Almost every building, particularly the Masonic Hall on the east side of the square, had been filled with ammunition, barrels of flour, cotton and medical stores. Emptying it and other buildings—particularly the Presbyterian church a block from the square—and piling the contents in the square and on adjacent streets was laborious and time consuming.

Before the Confederates emptied the Masonic Hall or the old hospital, the hall blew up. The powerful and deafening explosion did not obliterate the square. The courthouse survived for another two years.

The Presbyterian church in Holly Springs. Unfinished when the war broke out, Union troops used it as a stable and magazine. *Photograph by Garrie Colhoun.*

Old Hudsonville Road. The 1st Mississippi Cavalry rode down this road toward the fairgrounds; most of Van Dorn's command rode out of town on this road. *Photograph by Garrie Colhoun.*

The Presbyterian church still stands. But the General Hospital, on the west side, and the Magnolia Hotel, quarters for many Union officers, on the north side, perished.[275]

The total figures for about seven hours of destruction are staggering—even Grant's low figure of $400,000 worth of property destroyed. Other estimates ranged as high as $4,000,000. Van Dorn put the figure at $1,500,000, which is probably about right.[276]

Van Dorn's losses were nine killed and thirty-five wounded.[277]

By about 4:00 p.m., the work was done. Officers assembled their commands and prepared to ride out on the Hudsonville Road, headed north. Mrs. Mason, who had heard them coming, now saw them going. She marveled that "such a body of men, so ragged and worn, riding horses that were little better than skeletons should have conceived a feat so brilliant."[278]

Chapter 8

Lifelines and the "Rending Pain of Memory"

The dream of John S. Griffith was realized—the blow had been struck, and it only remained to be seen what effect it would have in causing the great Federal captain to change his plans for the reduction of Vicksburg.[279]

G rant conveyed the bad news from Holly Springs to Washington the next day. He soon learned that the day before Van Dorn rode into Holly Springs, Forrest had struck his lifeline farther north, tearing up sixty miles of track around Jackson, Tennessee.

In a dispatch to the "Commanding Officer Expedition Down Mississippi," Grant amplified his reaction to what had happened in his rear:

> *Raids made upon the railroad to my rear by Forrest northward from Jackson, and by Van Dorn northward from the Tallahatchie, have cut me off from supplies, so that farther advance by this route is perfectly impracticable....News received here from the south says that Vicksburg is now in our hands...These raids have cut off communication, so that I have had nothing from the north for over a week.*[280]

Grant had worked hard to ensure that Sherman would command the expedition downriver. Sherman's force left Memphis on the day of the raid in fifty-nine troop transports with seven gunboats. Grant, however, could not advance to support Sherman. He had halted his advance before the raid, but the raid had made it impossible for him to resume it. Van Dorn and his men knew nothing of this when they rode into Holly Springs, but their raid helped save Vicksburg in the sense that, because Grant could not support Sherman, the Confederates could reinforce Vicksburg from Grenada. When Pemberton learned from scouts and sympathizers along the river that Sherman was coming down in strength, he brought two brigades from Grenada to Vicksburg.[281] Sherman learned of the disaster at Holly Springs on the twenty-first but decided to go ahead. On December 26, Sherman began to disembark at landings on the Yazoo River, directly north of Vicksburg. The Confederates were prepared for him, and the subsequent result was a bloody defeat (Battle of Chickasaw Bayou, December 26–29). From the very beginning of the Mississippi Central campaign, the rumors and uncertainties about the expedition had been a vexing distraction to Grant, threatening unified command and clouding his strategic perspective. And now it had ended with Grant stalled on the Yalobusha and Sherman defeated on Chickasaw Bayou.

Taking stock on his own front, Grant saw that several of his officers had served him ill. Grant thought that Colonel Mizner of the 3rd Michigan Cavalry, at Water Valley, was to blame for Van Dorn riding out of Holly Springs unopposed. "I should feel insecure with you in command," he wrote to Mizner. Grant then ordered Mizner to turn his command over to Colonel Benjamin Grierson.[282] Grierson (1826–1911) would soon make his own mark as a raider. Grierson's Raid in the following spring figured significantly in Grant's next Vicksburg campaign.

Grant placed the blame for Van Dorn riding into Holly Springs squarely on Colonel Murphy. The day after the raid, Murphy submitted an exculpatory report, denying blame and praising his infantry, who fought very little, rather than his cavalry, who fought well. He said his force was inadequate. He claimed that the clearest warning that he received came from a "contraband" brought in very early on December 20 from Lumpkin's Mill. His claim raised more questions than it answered. In the words of one historian, it is "simply suspect" and "stuff and nonsense."[283]

Accurately, Murphy wrote, "My fate is most mortifying." Understandably, he added, "I have wished a hundred times to-day I had been killed."[284] He asked Grant for a personal interview, noting that he was "too unwell to leave my room except to avail of such a favor."[285]

Grant's headquarters responded with Special Field Orders condemning the "disgraceful surrender" of Holly Springs. Murphy had not taken "usual and necessary precautions." Even worse were the paroles. "The conduct of officers and men in accepting paroles under the circumstances is highly reprehensible and, to say the least, thoughtless."

Murphy's dismissal, dated from December 20, came on January 8.[286]

Distraction and incompetence aside, the campaign's undoing lay in its vulnerable line of supply. Cavalry—Forrest's and Van Dorn's—turned Grant back "without a major battle being fought."[287] Grant was well aware of Forrest's threat, but Van Dorn had surprised him.

After Holly Springs, Van Dorn, pursuant to orders, rode north. The element of surprise was gone, and he had some difficult days, especially at Davis' Mill on December 21 and at Middleburg, Tennessee, on December 24. But he reached Grenada on December 28 with his force intact, having ridden about five hundred miles in twelve days.[288]

Grant, by contrast, was hobbled. "I am now occupying the line of the Tallahatchie…waiting for communication to be opened," he wrote, "to know what move next to make."[289] There was no alternative to retreat, however: "To obtain supplies of forage I am gradually falling back to lines of Memphis and Corinth. Will leave Holly Springs about 10th."[290]

But Grant soon saw a silver lining, a lesson for the future that spelled Vicksburg's doom. With his stores destroyed, Grant turned on the Mississippi countryside for his supplies. "Since the late raids this department, except troops on the river, have subsisted off the country."[291] "I was amazed at the quantity of supplies the country afforded…we could have subsisted off the country for two months…this taught me a lesson…our loss of supplies was great at Holly Springs but it was more than compensated for by those taken from the country and the lesson taught…It could not be expected that men, with guns in their hands, would starve in the midst of plenty."[292]

A Union soldier wrote home on January 1, 1863, to say that Grant's policy was long overdue: "What he is doing now our whole army should

have done a year ago…Since the Raid we have drawn from the country…
All the stock and grain is taken…The inhabitants cannot subsist on what
we leave behind though we generally leave enough for immediate use. It
now looks like we are making war."[293]

The military winter of 1862–63 was a short one. The third Vicksburg
campaign—Grant's second—was only three months away. By that time,
the logistical and military situations had changed in significant ways.

On the day of the raid, Governor Pettus described the deteriorating
logistical situation to the state legislature in Jackson. He cited salt as a typical
example. Despite unlimited sources at New Iberia, Louisiana, Vicksburg
and the rest of the state were having to do without. The scant supplies on
hand would go to soldiers' families.[294] Then in April, Federal troops took
New Iberia. Even worse, by that time, the Federal navy had run the batteries
at Vicksburg twice more, "permanently cutting the flow of waterborne
supplies into the city."[295] Vicksburg's only lifeline now was the Southern
Railroad to Jackson. In the fall of 1862, it had been Grant who depended on
a vulnerable railroad to supply him. In the spring of 1863, it was Vicksburg.

Earl Van Dorn's situation had also changed. A week after the raid, the
Mobile Register and Advertiser saluted Van Dorn as "undoubtedly the right
man in the right place, and if he is permitted to retain command of our
cavalry he will make so far what has been one of the weakest aims…more
efficient and famous."[296]

Van Dorn's success animated his theater commander, General Joseph
E. Johnston. Johnston wanted to enlarge Van Dorn's command and
move him from Mississippi to Tennessee. On January 22, Johnston
informed Pemberton that he was combining all the cavalry in his and
Bragg's departments under Van Dorn. His mission would be to guard
Middle Tennessee and Mississippi and prevent any Federal troops from
moving from West Tennessee into Middle Tennessee.[297] In early March,
Van Dorn defeated a Union cavalry force at Thompson's Station, south
of Nashville. The next month, he was put in command of the Cavalry
Corps of the Army of Tennessee, with headquarters at Spring Hill. By
that time, the third Vicksburg campaign had begun.

On April 30, 1863, Grant crossed the Mississippi south of Vicksburg,
bringing his men from the Louisiana shore on troop transports that had

run by Vicksburg.[298] Grant intended to head northeast for Raymond, fifty miles away, aiming at Vicksburg's lifeline, the Southern Railroad of Mississippi. Grant had his own lifeline; Grand Gulf would be his base, where he would stockpile what he could not get from the countryside, i.e., ammunition, coffee, hard bread, sugar and salt. He could bring these up in wagons. For the rest, mainly beef and corn, he meant to live off the land.[299] On May 3, he telegraphed Halleck: "The country will supply all the forage required for anything like an active campaign, and the necessary fresh beef. Other supplies will have to be drawn…this is a long and precarious route, but I have every confidence in succeeding in doing it."[300]

Four days later, in Spring Hill, Tennessee, a jealous husband shot and killed Earl Van Dorn in his headquarters. What an end for the general who had silently pointed his sword at the enemy tents at Holly Springs, unleashing the charge that struck like a thunderbolt. Albert Castel has aptly written, "To this day his ghost must weep—he should have died leading a cavalry charge."[301] Instead, it was as General Johnston related in a letter he was writing when he was told the news of Van Dorn's death: "I have just been interrupted by a telegram which tells me that Major General Van Dorn, our first cavalry officer, was killed this morning by a Dr. Peters. It is a hard loss."[302] Dr. Peters ensured that Van Dorn did not live to see the surrender of the city he had defended so well.

Van Dorn was buried in Mount Vernon, Alabama, in his wife's family plot. In 1899, he was reinterred in his hometown of Port Gibson. His headstone bears no epitaph. The Confederate monument in Port Gibson, however, bears his likeness. He was an important figure, colorful and controversial, more known for Spring Hill than Holly Springs. His death on May 7 was immediately overshadowed by the death of Stonewall Jackson three days later. Jackson's impeccable, deeply religious character was beyond reproach. Van Dorn, by contrast, had admitted to Jefferson Davis that he was not a good Christian. But he became a good cavalryman. He is the subject of two excellent biographies by Arthur Carter and Robert Hartje. He left no memoir, however, not even a complete report of his raid on Holly Springs. Historians can only wish that Van Dorn had been a better historical source.

The Van Dorn of Vicksburg and the Van Dorn of Holly Springs have also been sources of literary inspiration. In August 1862, the South Carolina poet Paul Hamilton Hayne dedicated his "Vicksburg, a Ballad" to General Van Dorn. The poem first appeared in another city under siege, Charleston, in the *Daily Courier* on January 11, 1863. The first verse:

> *For sixty days and upward*
> *A storm of shell and shot*
> *Rained round us in a flowing shower*
> *But still we faltered not.*
> *"If the noble city perish,"*
> *Our bold young leader said,*
> *"Let the only walls the foe shall scale*
> *Be ramparts of the dead!"*[303]

The Van Dorn of Holly Springs loomed large in the life of William Faulkner (1897–1962) and in two of his great novels, *Sartoris* (1929) and *Light in August* (1932). Faulkner's hometown was New Albany, on the Tallahatchie. His great-grandfather, Colonel William C. Falkner, was the prototype of the fictional Colonel John Sartoris ("Cunnel"). Like Van Dorn, Falkner and Sartoris were cavalrymen. Like Van Dorn, they served briefly in Virginia before coming home to Mississippi. Falkner commanded the 1st Mississippi Partisan Rangers in North Mississippi in 1862. He sustained a bitter defeat on November 22 at the hands of Colonel Alfred Lee's 7th Kansas Cavalry south of Ripley. Lee reported that "Falkner with about 100 men escaped by dint of the hardest running...I consider Colonel Falkner's regiment now broken beyond any hope of reorganization."[304]

Like Van Dorn, after Corinth, Falkner felt the painful sting of defeat. Unlike Van Dorn, however, neither Falkner nor "Cunnel" ever experienced the redeeming moment of a Holly Springs.

In *Sartoris*, one of "Cunnel's" men tells how it was that Falkner was not part of that moment in history:

> *Van Dorn lit out one day headed nawth. Why, us boys didn't know...But Cunnel never had no idea of doin' that; his cawn hadn't*

been laid by yit…We knowed Van Dorn could handle 'em all right for a week or two. He usually done it…We'd been home two weeks and Cunnel had his cawn laid by when we heard 'bout Van Dorn ridin' into Holly Springs.[305]

In *Light in August*, the Reverend Gail Hightower's grandfather *was* with Van Dorn at Holly Springs—but *still* missed the ennobling glory of the moment. He was killed at Holly Springs, but not in Van Dorn's charge. Neither he nor Van Dorn died in a cavalry charge. Instead, Hightower was killed "with a shotgun, a fowling piece, in a hen house."[306]

The raid on Holly Springs never left his grandson's mind: "Riding for a hundred miles through a country where every grove and hamlet had its Yankee bivouac, and into a garrisoned town…here in the darkness, horses pulled short up…you see before the crash in the abrupt red glare the horses with wide eyes and nostrils in tossing heads."[307]

Sitting at his window every night, looking out on a back street in Faulkner's Jefferson, Mississippi, the rending memory never leaves him; he "still sees them; the wild bugles and the clashing sabers and the dying thunder of hooves."[308]

Notes

CHAPTER 1

1. Ballard, *Vicksburg*, 1–3; also Carter, *The Final Fortress*, 18; Groom, *Vicksburg 1863*, 149; and Shea and Winschel, *Vicksburg Is the Key*, 19.
2. Carter, *The Final Fortress*, 18.
3. Ibid., 21.
4. Ballard, *Vicksburg*, 8.
5. Ibid., 10.
6. Ibid., 12; also Cooper, *Jefferson Davis*, 328; also Long and Long, *The Civil War Day by Day*, 35–36.
7. For a masterful comparison of Confederate strengths and weaknesses, East and West, see Richard McMurray, *Two Great Rebel Armies* (Chapel Hill, University of North Carolina Press, 1989).
8. U.S. War Department, *War of the Rebellion: A Compilation of the Official Records of the Union and Confederate Armies*, ser. 1, vol. 10, part 2, 403. (All notations are from series 1 and cited henceforth as *O.R.*)
9. Carter, *The Final Fortress*, 35–36.
10. Perret, *Lincoln's War*, 110; see also Ballard, *Vicksburg*, 21.
11. Bishop, *Mississippi's Civil War Battlefields*, 231–32.

12. Duffy, *Lincoln's Admiral*, 176. The Vicksburg batteries today overlook the Yazoo Diversionary Canal.

13. Shea and Winschel, *Vicksburg Is the Key*, 17.

14. Wright, "Vicksburg and the Trans-Mississippi Supply Line," 211–15, passim.

15. Groom, *Vicksburg 1863*, 137.

16. Bearss, *Rebel Victory at Vicksburg*, 27.

17. Bergeron, "Mansfield Lovell," 45–71.

18. Shea and Winschel, *Vicksburg is the Key*, 18.

19. U.S. War Department, *War of the Rebellion: A Compilation of the Official Records of the Union and Confederate Navies*, ser. 1, vol. 18, 492. (All notations are from series 1 and cited henceforth as *O.R.N.*)

20. Bearss, *Rebel Victory*, 28; also Ballard, *Vicksburg*, 31.

21. *O.R.*, vol. 15, 754.

22. *O.R.*, vol. 52, part 2, 322; also Bergeron, "Mansfield Lovell," 57–58.

23. *O.R.*, vol. 17, part 2, 599.

24. *O.R.*, vol. 17, part 2, 613.

25. *O.R.*, vol. 17, part 2, 612.

26. Parson, "Thwarting Grant's First Drive on Vicksburg," 7.

27. Hartje, *Van Dorn*, 16–17.

28. Davis, *Rise and Fall*, vol. 2, 388.

29. Welsh, *Medical Histories*, 220.

30. Anon., "Hero of the Battle of Holly Springs," 71.

31. Dowdey, *Experiment in Rebellion*, 159.

32. Hartje, *Van Dorn*, 77.

33. Harwell, *The Confederate Reader*, 44–49.

34. Anon., "Hero of the Battle of Holly Springs," 71.

35. *O.R.*, vol. 8, 790; also Woodworth, *Jefferson Davis and His Generals*, 114–15.

36. Hartje, *Van Dorn*, 166–81.

37. See Hartje, *Van Dorn*, passim; also E. Miller, *A Soldier's Honor*, passim.

38. *O.R.*, vol. 52, part 2, 323–24.

39. Hartje, *Van Dorn*, 172. The author quoted from a letter from Pettus to Van Dorn, April 8, 1862, accompanying a presentation sword, incorrectly cited as part of the Van Dorn Collection at the Alabama

Department of Archives and History. The letter also is not found in the Mississippi Department of Archives and History. But it is too good a flourish to be left out. There is a copy of Hayne's poem in the Alabama Department of Archives and History Collection, as well as in Miller, *A Soldier's Honor*, and Moore, *Paul Hamilton Hayne*.

CHAPTER 2

40. Duffy, *Lincoln's Admiral*, 123.
41. Coombe, *Thunder along the Mississippi*, 149.
42. Parrish, *The Saga of the Confederate Ram "Arkansas,"* 148.
43. Coombe, *Thunder along the Mississippi*, 152.
44. Brown, I., "The Confederate Gun-Boat *Arkansas*," 572; also *O.R.*, vol. 52, part 2, 321; also *O.R.*, vol. 15, 767; also Parrish, *The Saga of the Confederate Ram "Arkansas,"* 141–48.
45. Read, "Reminiscences of the Confederate States Navy," 349.
46. *O.R.*, vol. 52, part 2, 322.
47. Still, "The Iron Rebel Navy," 28.
48. *O.R.*, vol. 15, 762–63.
49. Duffy, *Lincoln's Admiral*, 138.
50. *O.R.N.*, vol. 23, 243.
51. *O.R.*, vol. 52, part 2, 329.
52. Shea and Winschel, *Vicksburg Is the Key*, 21.
53. Duffy, *Lincoln's Admiral*, 128.
54. *O.R.*, vol. 15, 8.
55. *O.R.*, vol. 15, 14.
56. Groom, *Vicksburg 1863*, 151–52.
57. Bearss, "Armed Conflict," 453–54.
58. *O.R.N.*, vol. 18, 588.
59. Duffy, *Lincoln's Admiral*, 141; also Groom, *Vicksburg 1863*, 141.
60. Shea and Winschel, *Vicksburg Is the Key*, 20.
61. *O.R.*, vol. 15, 18, 761, 769–70.
62. *O.R.*, vol. 15, 766–67.
63. Hartje, *Van Dorn*, 192–96.

64. *O.R.*, vol. 15, 771–72.

65. *O.R.*, vol. 15, 15. On June 10, 1862, General Thomas C. Hindman placed Pulaski County (Little Rock), Arkansas, under martial law for the same reasons Van Dorn cited for his decree. See Neal and Kremm, *Lion of the South*, 121.

66. Gift, "The Story of the *Arkansas*," *SHSP*, and www.MissouriDivision-SCV.org.

67. Brown, "The Confederate Gun-Boat *Arkansas*," 572–73.

68. Bearss, *Rebel Victory*, 205; also S. Williams, "Missourians or Volunteers from Missouri Units," www.missouridivision-scv.org/mounits/cssark.htm.

69. Brown, "The Confederate Gun-Boat *Arkansas*," 573.

70. Groom, *Vicksburg 1863*, 154.

71. Gift, "The Story of the *Arkansas*," *SHSP*, and www.MissouriDivision-SCV.org.

72. Coombe, *Thunder along the Mississippi*, 154; also Brown, "The Confederate Gun-Boat *Arkansas*," 572.

73. Parrish, *The Saga of the Confederate Ram "Arkansas,"* 149.

74. *O.R.*, vol. 15, 1120–21.

75. Brown, "The Confederate Gun-Boat *Arkansas*," 573.

76. *O.R.*, vol. 52, part 2, 329.

77. *O.R.N.*, vol. 23, 243.

78. Brown, "The Confederate Gun-Boat *Arkansas*," 573.

79. Ballard, *Vicksburg*, 56; also Brown, "The Confederate Gun-Boat *Arkansas*," 574.

80. Read, "Reminiscences of the Confederate States Navy," 353.

81. Richard and Richard, *The Defense of Vicksburg*, 58–59.

82. *O.R.N.*, vol. 19, 68.

83. Brown, "The Confederate Gun-Boat *Arkansas*," 575.

84. Coleman, *A July Morning with the Rebel Ram "Arkansas,"* 8–9.

85. Brown, "The Confederate Gun-Boat *Arkansas*," 575–76.

86. Bearss, *Rebel Victory*, 219.

87. Duffy, *Lincoln's Admiral*, 143.

88. Bagart letter (July 17, 1862).

89. Duffy, *Lincoln's Admiral*, 145.

90. Read, "Reminiscences of the Confederate States Navy," 354.

91. *O.R.N.*, vol. 23, 244.

92. Brown, "The Confederate Gun-Boat *Arkansas*," 575–76.

93. Bearss, *Rebel Victory*, 222.

94. Ibid., 224.

95. Shea and Winschel, *Vicksburg Is the Key*, 25.

96. Richard and Richard, *The Defense of Vicksburg*, 59.

97. *O.R.N.*, vol. 19, 64–65.

98. Young, *Reminiscences of a Soldier of the Orphan Brigade*, 77–78.

99. Gift, "The Story of the Arkansas," *SHSP*, and www.MissouriDivision-SCV.org.

100. *O.R.*, vol. 15, 16.

101. Groom, *Vicksburg 1863*, 158.

102. Gift, "The Story of the Arkansas," *SHSP*, and www.MissouriDivision-SCV.org.

103. Ballard, *Vicksburg*, 58. Ballard cites *Official Records of the Union and Confederate Navies* 19:69, 133; I.E. Fiske to John Comstock, July 24, 1862, Comstock Papers, University of North Carolina at Chapel Hill.

104. Williams, "Letters of General Thomas Williams," 324.

105. *O.R.N.*, vol. 23, 267.

106. Brown, "The Confederate Gun-Boat *Arkansas*," 577.

107. *O.R.*, vol. 52, part 2, 329.

108. Bearss, *Rebel Victory*, 148.

109. Ibid., 230.

110. Young, *Reminiscences of a Soldier of the Orphan Brigade*, 37–39.

111. *O.R.N.*, vol. 19, 72.

112. Ibid.

113. Ibid., 260.

114. Brown, "The Confederate Gun-Boat *Arkansas*," 578.

115. Bearss, *Rebel Victory*, 268.

116. *O.R.*, vol. 52, part 2, 332.

117. *O.R.*, vol. 52, part 2, 331.

118. *O.R.*, vol. 15, 16.

119. *O.R.*, vol. 15, 16; also Winters, *The Civil War in Louisiana*, 166; also Hewitt, *Port Hudson*, Preface, 1–6.

120. *O.R.*, vol. 15, 76–77.

121. *O.R.N.*, vol. 19, 71.

122. Brown, "The Confederate Gun-Boat *Arkansas*," 574.

123. Read, "Reminiscences of the Confederate States Navy," 359.

124. *O.R.*, vol. 15, 17.

125. Brown, "The Confederate Gun-Boat *Arkansas*," 578–79.

126. *O.R.N.*, vol. 19, 122.

127. Read, "Reminiscences of the Confederate States Navy," 360–61.

128. Parrish, *The Saga of the Confederate Ram "Arkansas,"* 147.

129. *O.R.*, vol. 15, 18.

130. Parrish, *The Saga of the Confederate Ram "Arkansas,"* 198.

131. Bearss, "Armed Conflict," 455; also Davis, *Breckinridge*, 324.

132. Wright, "Vicksburg and the Trans-Mississippi Supply Line," 213–17; author cites *O.R.*, vol. 24, part 3, 591, and *O.R.*, series 4, vol. 2, 126.

133. Smith, "Major General Mansfield Lovell," 8.

CHAPTER 3

134. *O.R.*, vol. 17, part 2, 656; also Groom, *Vicksburg 1863*, 169.

135. *O.R.*, vol. 17, part 2, 700.

136. Bearss, "Armed Conflict," 456–57.

137. Maury, "Recollections of Campaigns against Grant," 302.

138. Crist, *The Papers of Jefferson Davis*, vol. 8, 434.

139. *O.R.*, vol. 17, part 2, 726–27.

140. Crist, *The Papers of Jefferson Davis*, vol. 8, 452.

141. *O.R.*, vol. 17, part 2, 727.

142. *O.R.*, vol. 17, part 1, 381.

143. Osborne, ed., "The Civil War Letters of Robert W. Banks," 147–48.

144. Crist, *The Papers of Jefferson Davis*, vol. 8, 436.

145. Miller, *A Soldier's Honor*, 322–23.

146. *O.R.*, vol. 17, part 1, 414–59 (Record of Court of Inquiry).

147. Crist, *The Papers of Jefferson Davis*, vol. 8, 480.

148. *O.R.*, vol. 17, part 1, 459 (Record of Court of Inquiry).

149. Hartje, *Van Dorn*, 262–65.

150. *O.R.*, vol. 17, part 2, 788–92. Phelan's letter was a long description and analysis of the overall situation in Mississippi. Van Dorn was its first topic.

151. Crist, *The Papers of Jefferson Davis*, vol. 8, 537–38.

152. Lowry, *Tarnished Eagles*, 176.

153. Ibid., 179.

154. Ibid., 176; also Parson, "Thwarting Grant's First Drive on Vicksburg," 19.

155. Osborne, ed., "The Civil War Letters of Robert W. Banks," 143.

156. Parson, "Thwarting Grant's First Drive on Vicksburg," 19; also Lowry, *Curmudgeons, Drunkards, and Outright Fools*, 176–81; also Commager, *The Civil War Archive*, 331; also Politzer, "Robert Creighton Murphy," 4.

Chapter 4

157. Loughborough, *My Cave Life in Vicksburg*, 175.

158. Hamilton, *Holly Springs, Mississippi*, 10; also Shipp, *Windows to Holly Springs*, 11–16; also Mickle, "Van Dorn Raid," marshallcountyms.org/military/vandorn.php.

159. Stewart, "From Whence We Came," www.southreporter.com/2005/wk15/features/html.

160. Miller, *Lost Landmarks of Mississippi*, 144–45; also Shipp, *Windows to Holly Springs*, 30–31; also Cauthen, *Mississippi's Railroad Heritage*, 100–1; also Hamilton, *Holly Springs, Mississippi*, 61.

161. Black, *The Railroads of the Confederacy*, 1.

162. Miller, *Lost Landmarks of Mississippi*, 141–45.

163. For the disaster at Duck Hill, see Wynne, *Mississippi's Civil War* and Ezell, "Tragedy at Duck Hill Station," genealogytrails.com/miss/montgomery/trainwreck.html.

164. Fletcher Pomeroy diary, with permission of Don Paul.

165. Parks, "One Story of the 109th Illinois Volunteer Infantry Regiment," 289.

Chapter 5

166. Ballard, *Vicksburg*, 87.

167. *O.R.*, vol. 52, part 2, 354.

168. *O.R.*, vol. 17, part 2, 728.

169. *O.R.*, vol. 17, part 2, 735; also Williams, "Last Chance to Save Vicksburg," 6–19.

170. Shea and Winschel, *Vicksburg Is the Key*, 35–36; also Bearss, *The Campaign for Vicksburg*, vol. 1, 29–34; also Parson, "Thwarting Grant's First Drive on Vicksburg,"18–19.

171. *O.R.*, vol. 17, part 1, 466–67.

172. Ballard, *Vicksburg*, 85.

173. *O.R.*, vol. 17, part 2, 322.

174. *O.R.*, vol. 17, part 1, 468.

175. *O.R.*, vol. 17, part 2, 348.

176. Mason, "Raid on Holly Springs," *Memphis Commercial Appeal*.

177. Loughborough, *My Cave Life in Vicksburg*, 175–79; also Bearss, *The Campaign for Vicksburg*, vol. 1, 50–51.

178. *O.R.*, vol. 17, part 2, 746.

179. *O.R.*, vol. 17, part 1, 488–90.

180. Ballard, *Vicksburg*, 101–2.

181. *O.R.*, vol. 17, part 1, 469–71; *O.R.*, vol. 17, part 2, 348.

182. *O.R.*, vol. 17, part 1, 469.

183. Bearss, *The Campaign for Vicksburg*, vol. 1, 72–73.

184. Mason, "Raid on Holly Springs," *Memphis Commercial Appeal*.

185. Aiken, *William Faulkner and the Southern Landscape*, 101; also www.walterplace.com/TheHistory/history.html.

186. *O.R.*, vol. 17, part 2, 380.

187. *O.R.*, vol. 17, part 2, 750.

188. *O.R.*, vol. 17, part 1, 468; *O.R.*, vol. 17, part 2, 745.

189. Ballard, *Vicksburg*, 101–3.

190. *O.R.*, vol. 17, part 2, 771.

191. *O.R.*, vol. 17, part 2, 772.

192. Hubbard, *Notes of a Private*, 54.

193. Osborne, ed., "The Civil War Letters of Robert W. Banks," 153.

194. *O.R.*, vol. 17, part 2, 779.

195. Ballard, *Vicksburg*, 104.

196. Anon., "The Mississippi Central Railroad Campaign," www. angelfire.com/ms2/grantshilohvicksburg.

197. *O.R.*, vol. 17, part 2, 779.

198. *O.R.*, vol. 7, part 1, 471–72.

199. Anon., "The Mississippi Central Railroad Campaign," www. angelfire.com/ms2/grantshilohvicksburg.

200. *O.R.*, vol. 17, part 1, 503.

201. Bearss, *The Campaign for Vicksburg*, vol. 1, 107.

202. Ballard, *Vicksburg*, 118–19; also Hale, *Third Texas Cavalry*, 142; also Shea and Winschel, *Vicksburg Is the Key*, 38, and "The Mississippi Central Railroad Campaign," www.angelfire.com/ms2/grantshilohvicksburg.

203. *O.R.*, vol. 7, part 1, 471–72.

204. *O.R.*, vol. 17, part 1, 473.

205. Bearss, *The Campaign for Vicksburg*, vol. 1, 107–11, passim.

206. *O.R.*, vol. 17, part 1, 475.

207. Bearss, *The Campaign for Vicksburg*, vol. 1, 294.

208. *O.R.*, vol. 17, part 2, 424. When Halleck learned of these orders on January 9, he revoked them.

209. Cramer, ed., *Letters of Ulysses S. Grant*, 96–97.

CHAPTER 6

210. Williams, "Last Chance to Save Vicksburg," 8.

211. Skates, "James Phelan," 1204–5.

212. *O.R.*, vol. 17, part 2, 789.

213. Ibid., 788–92.

214. Williams, "Last Chance to Save Vicksburg," 14.

215. Allardice, *More Generals in Gray*, 106–7; also Sparks, *The War Between the States as I Saw It*, 333.

216. Parson, "Thwarting Grant's First Drive on Vicksburg," 8; also Bearss, *The Campaign for Vicksburg*, vol. 1, 47–49, and *O.R.*, vol. 17, part 2, 738.

217. For an accurate characterization, see Ballard, *Vicksburg*, 119–20; for the complete text, see Parson, "Thwarting Grant's First Drive on Vicksburg," 6.

218. Parson, "Thwarting Grant's First Drive on Vicksburg," 6.

219. Hughes, *Liddell's Record*, 65–66.

220. Bearss, *The Campaign for Vicksburg*, vol. 1, 291.

221. Carter, *The Final Fortress*, 129.

222. Parson, "Thwarting Grant's First Drive on Vicksburg," 27.

223. Maury, "Recollections of Earl Van Dorn," 196.

224. Brown, "Van Dorn's Operations in Northern Mississippi," 155.

225. Stevenson, "The Capture of Holly Springs," 134.

226. Chadwell, unpublished diary, by permission of Susan Chadwell Dignard and the Chadwell family descendants, and with thanks to Kenneth Hurt and Robert Schmidt, August 18 entry; see also Schmidt, *"Boys of the Best Families in the State"*; also Hartje, "Van Dorn Conducts a Raid," 120–33, 123–24; also Carter, *The Tarnished Cavalier*, 130.

227. Chadwell diary, December 15.

228. Parson, "Thwarting Grant's First Drive on Vicksburg," 9.

229. Carter, *The Final Fortress*, 130–31; also Chadwell diary, December 15; also Kerr, ed., *Fighting with Ross' Texas Cavalry Brigade*, 50–52.

230. Kerr, ed., *Fighting with Ross' Texas Cavalry Brigade*, 51.

231. Chadwell diary, December 18.

232. Lowe, *A Texas Cavalry Officer's Civil War*, 219; also Parson, "Thwarting Grant's First Drive on Vicksburg," 9.

233. Thomas, ed., *Three Years with Grant*, 34–35; also Carter, *The Final Fortress*, 132–35.

234. *O.R.*, vol. 17, part 1, 499.

235. Parson, "Thwarting Grant's First Drive on Vicksburg," 12.

236. *O.R.*, vol. 17, part 2, 435–40.

237. Parson, "Thwarting Grant's First Drive on Vicksburg," 27.

238. *O.R.*, vol. 17, part 1, 512–13; also Hartje, "Van Dorn Conducts a Raid," 126.

239. Parson, "Thwarting Grant's First Drive on Vicksburg," 20 and Map Section; also Brown, "Van Dorn's Operations in Northern Mississippi, 155–57; also Carter, *The Final Fortress*, 133–34; also Deupree, "The

Noxubee Squadrons," 53–54; Hale, *The Third Texas Cavalry*, 145; Lowe, *A Texas Cavalry Officer's Civil War*, 215; Kerr, ed., *Fighting with Ross' Texas Cavalry Brigade*, 51.

240. *O.R.*, vol. 17, part 2, 444.
241. Chadwell diary, December 20.
242. Stevenson, "The Capture of Holly Springs," 134.
243. Crabb, *All Afire to Fight*, 137.
244. Brown, "Van Dorn's Operations in Northern Mississippi," 157.

CHAPTER 7

245. Mason, "Raid on Holly Springs," *Memphis Commercial Appeal*.
246. Hubbard, *Notes of a Private*, 56.
247. Chadwell diary, December 20.
248. Parson, "Thwarting Grant's First Drive on Vicksburg," 21–22.
249. Mason, "Raid on Holly Springs," *Memphis Commercial Appeal*.
250. *O.R.*, vol. 17, part 1, 516.
251. Crabb, *All Afire to Fight*, 133–34.
252. Brown, "Van Dorn's Operations in Northern Mississippi," 158.
253. McMinn, "Service with Van Dorn's Cavalry," 385.
254. Deupree, "The Noxubee Squadrons," 62.
255. Chadwell diary, December 20.
256. Parson, "Thwarting Grant's First Drive on Vicksburg," 24.
257. *O.R.*, vol. 17, part 1, 512–13.
258. Crabb, *All Afire to Fight*, 134.
259. Parson, "Thwarting Grant's First Drive on Vicksburg," 42.
260. Hale, *The Third Texas Cavalry*, 146; also Rose, *Ross' Texas Brigade*, 87–90, and McMinn, "Service with Van Dorn's Cavalry," 385.
261. Deupree, "The Noxubee Squadrons," 61–62.
262. Ibid., 62.
263. Scott, *Four Years Service in the Southern Army*, 20.
264. Hubbard, *Notes of a Private*, 57.
265. Lowe, *A Texas Cavalry Officer's Civil War*, 220–21.
266. Crabb, *All Afire to Fight*, 137; also see Rose, *Ross' Texas Brigade*, 87–88.

267. Bearss, *The Campaign for Vicksburg*, vol. 1, 317.

268. *O.R.*, vol. 17, part 2, 443.

269. *Missouri Democrat*, "Particulars of the Rebel Raid into Holly Springs."

270. *O.R.*, vol. 17, part 2, 380.

271. Barron, *The Lone Star Defenders*, 455.

272. Hillyer letter, 1862.

273. *O.R.*, vol. 17, part 1, 510–11.

274. Hillyer letter, 1862.

275. Roth and Parson, "The Generals Tour," 51–65.

276. *O.R.*, vol. 17, part 1, 503; also Carter, *The Final Fortress*, 145, and Bearss, *The Campaign for Vicksburg*, vol. 1, 317.

277. Parson, "Thwarting Grant's First Drive on Vicksburg," 44.

278. Mason, "Raid on Holly Springs," *Memphis Commercial Appeal*. Some of Van Dorn's men may have left on the La Grange Road.

CHAPTER 8

279. Sparks, *The War Between the States as I Saw It*, 211.

280. *O.R.*, vol. 17, part 2, 463.

281. Bearss, *The Campaign for Vicksburg*, vol. 1, 149–50.

282. *O.R.*, vol. 17, part 2, 448.

283. *O.R.*, vol. 17, part 2, 444; also Parson, "Thwarting Grant's First Drive on Vicksburg," 20–21.

284. *O.R.*, vol. 17, part 1, 509.

285. Simon, ed., *The Papers of Ulysses S. Grant*, vol. 7, 106.

286. *O.R.*, vol. 17, part 1, 515–16. Murphy found employment in the Department of Agriculture and then as a postal clerk. In 1863, he tried to have his arrest and dismissal rescinded. Lincoln sent his appeal, which came by way of the Wisconsin State Assembly, to Judge Advocate General Joseph Hill. On May 30, Hill ruled favorably on the appeal, but nothing was ever done. Murphy gave up trying in 1880, when a bill "For the Relief of Robert C. Murphy" was allowed to die in the Senate's Military Affairs Committee. Murphy died in 1888 and was buried in an unmarked grave in his wife's family plot in the

Congressional Cemetery in Washington, D.C. See Politzer, "Robert Creighton Murphy," 4; also Parson, "Thwarting Grant's First Drive on Vicksburg," 49.

287. Ballard, *Vicksburg*, 256.

288. Lowe, *A Texas Cavalry Officer's Civil War*, 217.

289. *O.R.*, vol. 17, part 1, 478.

290. *O.R.*, vol. 17, part 1, 481.

291. *O.R.*, vol. 17, part 1, 480.

292. Long, ed., *Personal Memoirs of U.S. Grant*, 226–27.

293. "Clint to Hannah" letter, January 1, 1863.

294. Wright, "Vicksburg and the Trans-Mississippi Supply Line," 217, 223. The author cites *O.R.*, series 4, vol. 2, 126, 250.

295. Wright, "Vicksburg and the Trans-Mississippi Supply Line," 224.

296. *Mobile Register and Advertiser*, December 27, 1862.

297. *O.R.*, vol. 17, part 2, 808, 811–13, 832–33.

298. Kyle, "Grant, Meade and Clausewitz," 21–27.

299. Hills, "Grant's Vicksburg Supply Line: Myth or Fact?" civilwar.org/battlefields/vicksburg/vicksburg-history-articles/vicksburgsupplyhillpg.html.

300. *O.R.*, vol. 24, part 1, 32–33; also Bearss, *The Campaign for Vicksburg*, vol. 2, 435.

301. Castel, *Articles of War*, 113.

302. Hughes, "Some War Letters of General Joseph E. Johnston," 320.

303. Moore, *Paul Hamilton Hayne*, 52; also Miller, *A Soldier's Honor*, 74–80.

304. *O.R.*, vol. 17, part 1, 490–91.

305. Faulkner, *Sartoris*, 185.

306. Ibid., 459.

307. Faulkner, *Light in August*, 457–59.

308. Ibid., 467.

Bibliography

BOOKS

Aiken, Charles S. *William Faulkner and the Southern Landscape*. Athens: University of Georgia Press, 2009.

Allardice, Bruce S. *More Generals in Gray*. Baton Rouge: Louisiana State University Press, 1995.

Ballard, Michael B. "Misused Merit: The Tragedy of John C. Pemberton." In *Civil War Generals in Defeat*, edited by Steven E. Woodworth. Lawrence: University of Kansas Press, 1999, 141–61.

———. *U.S. Grant: The Making of a General 1861–1863*. London: Roman and Littlefield Publishers, 2005.

———. *Vicksburg: The Campaign That Opened the Mississippi*. Chapel Hill: University of North Carolina Press, 2004.

Barron, S.B. *The Lone Star Defenders: A Chronicle of the Third Texas Cavalry, Ross' Brigade*. New York: The Neale Publishing Co., 1908.

Bearss, Edwin C. "The Armed Conflict, 1861–1865." In *A History of Mississippi*, edited by R.A. McLemore. Vol. 1. Jackson: Jackson University and College Press of Mississippi, 1973, 447–92.

———. *The Campaign for Vicksburg*. Vols. 1–2. Dayton, OH: Morningside House, Inc., 1985, 1986.

———. *Rebel Victory at Vicksburg*. Vicksburg Centennial Commemoration Commission. Little Rock, AR: Pioneer Press, 1963.

Bergeron, A.W. "Mansfield Lovell." *In Confederate Generals in the Western Theater*, edited by L.L. Hewitt and A.W. Bergeron. Vol. 1. Knoxville: University of Tennessee Press, 2010, 45–71. (In vol. 2 of this work, chapter three is an essay by Charles Elliot on General Van Dorn's Baton Rouge campaign. I was not aware of it until too late and have not seen it.)

Bishop, Randy. *Mississippi's Civil War Battlefields*. Gretna, LA: Pelican Publishing Co., 2010.

Black, Robert C., III. *The Railroads of the Confederacy*. Chapel Hill: University of North Carolina Press, 1952.

Brieger, James F. *Hometown Mississippi: An Early Settlement History of Over 3300 Places in the State*. N.p., 1960.

Brown, Isaac Newton, Captain. "The Confederate Gun-Boat *Arkansas*." In *Battles and Leaders of the Civil War*, vol. 3, edited by Robert Underwood Johnson and Clarence Clough Buel. New York: Thomas Yoseloff, Inc., 1956, 572–79.

Carter, Arthur B. *The Tarnished Cavalier: Major General Earl Van Dorn, C.S.A.* Knoxville: University of Tennessee Press, 1990.

Carter, Samuel, III. *The Final Fortress: The Campaign for Vicksburg 1862–1863*. New York: St. Martin's Press, 1980.

Castel, Albert. *Articles of War: Winners, Losers, and Some Who Were Both during the Civil War*. Mechanicsburg, PA: Stackpole Books, 2001.

Cauthen, Sharron D. *Mississippi's Railroad Heritage*. Madison, MS: China Lamp Publishing., n.d.

Clark, Olynthus B., ed. *Downing's Civil War Diary*. Des Moines: History Department of Iowa, 1916.

Coleman, S.B. *A July Morning with the Rebel Ram "Arkansas."* Little Rock, AR: Eagle Press, and Detroit: Wine and Hammond Press, 1896.

Commager, Henry Steele. *The Civil War Archive: The History of the Civil War in Documents*. New York: Black Dog Publishing, 2000.

Coombe, Jack D. *Thunder Along the Mississippi: The River Battles That Split the Confederacy*. New York: Sarpedon Publishers, 1996.

Cooper, William J. *Jefferson Davis: American*. New York: A.A. Knopf, 2000.

Cozzens, Peter. *The Darkest Days of the War: The Battles of Iuka and Corinth.* Chapel Hill: University of North Carolina Press, 1997.

Crabb, Martha L. *All Afire to Fight: The Untold Tale of the Civil War's Ninth Texas Cavalry.* New York: Avon Books, 2000.

Cramer, Jessie Grant, ed. *Letters of Ulysses S. Grant to His Father and Youngest Sister, 1857–78.* New York: G.P. Putnam's Sons, 1912.

Crist, Lynda L., ed. *The Papers of Jefferson Davis: January–September 1863.* Vol. 8. Baton Rouge: Louisiana State University Press, 1997.

Davis, Jefferson. *The Rise and Fall of the Confederate Government.* Vol. 2. New York: D. Appleton & Company, 1881.

Davis, William C. *Breckinridge: Statesman, Soldier, Symbol.* Baton Rouge: Louisiana State University Press, 1974.

Dowdey, Clifford. *Experiment in Rebellion.* Garden City, NY: Doubleday & Co., 1946.

Duffy, James P. *Lincoln's Admiral: The Civil War Campaigns of David Farragut.* New York: John Wiley & Sons, 1997.

Faulkner, William. *Light in August.* New York: Modern Library, 1959.

———. *Sartoris.* New York: American Library, 1964.

Faust, Patricia L., ed. *Historical Times Illustrated Encyclopedia of the Civil War.* New York: Harper & Row Publishers, 1986.

Groom, Winston. *Vicksburg 1863.* New York: Random House, Inc., 2010.

Hale, Douglas. *The Third Texas Cavalry in the Civil War.* Norman: University of Oklahoma, 1993.

Hamilton, William Baskerville. *Holly Springs, Mississippi, to the Year 1878.* Holly Springs, MS: Marshall County Historical Society/Bailey Printing Co., 1984.

Hartje, Robert G. *Van Dorn: The Life and Times of a Confederate General.* Nashville, TN: Vanderbilt University Press, 1967.

Harwell, Richard B. *The Confederate Reader.* New York: Longmans, Greer & Co., 1957.

Hewitt, Lawrence L. *Port Hudson: Confederate Bastion on the Mississippi.* Baton Rouge: Louisiana State University Press, 1987.

Howell, Elmo. *Mississippi Back Roads: Notes on Literature and History.* Memphis, TN: Langford & Associates, 1998.

Hubbard, John Milton. *Notes of a Private*. St. Louis, MO: Nixon-Jones Publishing Co., 1911.

Hughes, Nathaniel C., ed. *Liddell's Record: St. John Richardson Liddell*. Baton Rouge: Louisiana State University Press, 1985.

Jones, Archer. *Confederate Strategy from Shiloh to Vicksburg*. Baton Rouge: Louisiana State University Press, 1991.

Keegan, John. "Grant and Unheroic Leadership" in *The Mask of Command*. New York: Viking Adult, 1987.

Keen, Newton A. *Living and Fighting with the Texas 6th Cavalry*. Gaithersburg, MD: Butternut Press, Inc., 1986.

Kerr, Homer L., ed. *Fighting with Ross' Texas Cavalry Brigade, C.S.A.: The Diary of George L. Griscom, Adjutant, 9th Texas Cavalry Regiment*. Hillsdale, TX: Hill Jr. College Press, 1976.

Key, Hobart, and Max S. Lale, eds. *The Civil War Letters of David R. Garrett: Detailing the Adventures of the 6th Texas Cavalry 1861–1865*. Marshall, TX: Port Caddo Press, 1963.

Klement, Frank L. *Wisconsin in the Civil War*. Madison: State Historical Society of Wisconsin, 1997.

Konstam, Angus. *Mississippi River Gunboats of the American Civil War 1861–1865*. Oxford: Osprey Publishing Ltd., 2002.

Long, E.B., ed. *Personal Memoirs of U.S. Grant*. New York: Grosset & Dunlap, 1962.

Long, E.B., and Barbara Long. *The Civil War Day by Day: An Almanac*. Garden City, NY: Doubleday & Company, Inc., 1972.

Loughborough, Mary Ann Webster. *My Cave Life in Vicksburg*. (Previously published 1864, 1882.) Wilmington, NC: Broadfoot Publishing Co., 1989.

Lowe, Richard, ed. *A Texas Cavalry Officer's Civil War: The Diary and Letters of James C. Bates*. Baton Rouge: Louisiana State University Press, 1999.

Lowry, Thomas P. *Curmudgeons, Drunkards, and Outright Fools: Courts-Martial of Civil War Union Generals*. Lincoln: University of Nebraska Press, 1997.

———. *Tarnished Eagles: The Courts-Martial of Fifty Union Colonels and Lieutenant Colonels*. Mechanicsburg, PA: Stackpole Books, 1997.

Miller, Emily Van Dorn. *A Soldier's Honor, With Reminiscences of Major-General Earl Van Dorn*. New York: Abbey Press, 1902. Also Kessinger Publishing's Rare Imprints.

Miller, Mary Carol. *Lost Landmarks of Mississippi*. Jackson: University Press of Mississippi, 2002.

Moore, Rayburn S. *Paul Hamilton Hayne*. New York: Twagne Publications, Inc., 1972.

Neal, Diane, and Thomas W. Kremm. *Lion of the South: General Thomas C. Hindman*. Macon, GA: Mercer University Press, 1993.

Parrish, Tom Z. *The Saga of the Confederate Ram "Arkansas": The Mississippi Valley Campaign, 1862*. Hillsboro, TX: Hill College Press, 1987.

Perret, Geoffrey. *Lincoln's War*. New York: Random House, 2004.

Richard, Allen C., Jr., and Mary Margaret Higginbotham Richard. *The Defense of Vicksburg: A Louisiana Chronicle*. College Station: Texas A&M University Press, 2004.

Rose, Victor M. *Ross' Texas Brigade: Being a Narrative of Events Connected with Its Service in the Late War Between the States*. Louisville, KY: Courier-Journal Company, 1881.

Rowland, Dunbar. *Military History of Mississippi 1803–1898*. Spartanburg, SC: Reprint Company, 1978.

Schmidt, Bob. *"Boys of the Best Families in the State": Co. E., 2nd Missouri Confederate Cavalry*. French Village, MO: Two Trails Publishing, 2002.

Scott, Joe M. *Four Years Service in the Southern Army*. Edited by W.J. Lemke. Originally published Mulberry, AR: Leader Office Printers, 1897. Repr., Fayetteville, AR: Washington County Historical Society, 1959.

Shaw, David W. *Sea Wolf of the Confederacy: The Daring Civil War Raids of Naval Lt. Charles W. Read*. New York: Free Press, 2004.

Shea, William L., and Terrence J. Winshel. *Vicksburg Is the Key: The Struggle for the Mississippi River*. Lincoln: University of Nebraska Press, 2003.

Shipp, Lois Swanee. *Windows to Holly Springs: History and Her Culinary Delights*. Florence, MS: Stephens Printing Co., 2003. For Marshall County Historical Museum.

Simon, John Y., ed. *The Papers of Ulysses S. Grant*. Carbondale: Southern Illinois University Press, 1967.

———, ed. *The Personal Memoirs of Julia Dent Grant (Mrs. Ulysses S. Grant)*. New York: G.P. Putnam's Sons, 1975.

Skates, Ray. "James Phelan." In *Encyclopedia of the Confederacy*, edited by Richard Current, vol. 3, 1204–5. New York: Simon & Schuster, 1999.

Sparks, A.W. *The War Between the States as I Saw It: Reminiscent, Historical, and Personal.* Tyler, TX: Lee & Burnett, 1901. Reprinted as *Recollections of the Great War*, Longview, TX: D&D Publishing, 1987.

Thomas, Benjamin T., ed. *Three Years with Grant as Recalled by War Correspondent Sylvanus Cadwallader.* New York: A.A. Knopf, 1956.

Turner, George E. *Victory Rode the Rails: The Strategic Place of the Railroads in the Civil War.* Lincoln: University of Nebraska Press, 1992, 1997.

U.S. War Department. *War of the Rebellion: A Compilation of the Official Records of the Union and Confederate Armies.* 128 vols. (Only the following Series 1 volumes were used in this book: Vols. 8, 10 (part 2), 15, 17 (parts 1, 2), 24 (part 1), 52 (part 2).) Washington, D.C.: Government Printing Office, 1880–1901.

———. *War of the Rebellion: A Compilation of the Official Records of the Union and Confederate Navies.* 30 vols. (Only the following Series 1 volumes were used in this book: Vols. 18, 19, 23.) Washington, D.C.: Government Printing Office, 1894–1922.

Wakelyn, Jon L., and Frank E. Vandiver. *Biographical Dictionary of the Confederacy.* Westport, CT: Greenwood Press, 1977.

Walker, Peter F. *Vicksburg: A People at War 1860–1865.* Chapel Hill: University of North Carolina Press, 1960.

Warner, Ezra J. *Generals in Gray: Lives of the Confederate Commanders.* Baton Rouge: Louisiana State University Press, 1959.

Welsh, Jack D., MD. *Medical Histories of Confederate Generals.* Kent, OH: Kent State University Press, 1995.

Williamson, Joel. *William Faulkner and Southern History.* New York: Oxford University Press, 1993.

Winschel, Terrence J. *Triumph and Defeat: The Vicksburg Campaign.* Mason City, IA: Savas Publishing Co., 1999.

Winters, John D. *The Civil War in Louisiana.* Baton Rouge: Louisiana State University Press, 1963.

Woodworth, Steven E. *Jefferson Davis and His Generals: The Failure of Confederate Command in the West.* Lawrence: University Press of Kansas, 1990.

Wynne, Ben. *Mississippi's Civil War: A Narrative History.* Mercer, GA: Mercer University Press, 2006.

Young, J.P. *The Seventh Tennessee Cavalry (Confederate): A History*. Nashville, TN: Church & Sons, 1890.

Young, L.D., Lieut. *Reminiscences of a Soldier of the Orphan Brigade*. Paris, KY: Job Printing Company, 1918. Printed for the *Louisville Courier-Journal*.

JOURNAL ARTICLES

Anon. "At the Crossroads: Northeast Mississippi in the Civil War." *Northeast Mississippi Daily Journal* (April 24, 2011).

Anon. "General Earl Van Dorn Captures Holly Springs." *Tombigbee Country Magazine* 53 (July 2004): 51–54.

Anon. "General Earl Van Dorn: Hero of the Battle of Holly Springs." *Tombigbee Country Magazine* 57 (October 2004): 68–71.

Brown, A.F., Colonel. "Van Dorn's Operations in Northern Mississippi: Recollections of a Cavalryman." *Southern Historical Society Papers* 6 (July–December 1878): 151–61.

Brown, S.H. "Van Dorn at Holly Springs." *Confederate Veteran* 10 (October 1892): 455–56.

Deupree, J.G. "The Capture of Holly Springs, Mississippi, December 20, 1862." *Publications of the Mississippi Historical Society* 4 (1901): 49–62.

———. "The Noxubee Squadrons of the First Mississippi Cavalry, C.S.A., 1861–1865." *Publications of the Mississippi Historical Society* (Centenary series) 2 (1918): 12–143.

Gift, George W. "The Story of the *Arkansas*." *Southern Historical Society Papers* 12, nos. 1, 2 (January 1884, February 1884): 205–12.

Hartje, Robert. "Van Dorn Conducts a Raid on Holly Springs and Eastern Tennessee." *Tennessee Historical Quarterly* 18 (June 1959): 120–33.

Hughes, Robert M. "Some War Letters of General Joseph E. Johnston." *Journal of the Military Service Institution of the United States* (May–June 1912): 318–28.

Kyle, Robert K., Jr. "Grant, Meade and Clausewitz: The Application of War as an Extension of Policy during the Vicksburg and Gettysburg Campaigns." *Army History* 28 (Fall 1993): 21–27.

Maury, Dabney H. "Grant's Campaign in North Mississippi." *Southern Magazine* 13 (July–December 1875): 410–17.

———. "Recollections of Campaigns against Grant in North Mississippi in 1861–1863." *Southern Historical Society Papers* 13 (January–December 1885): 285–311.

———. "Recollections of General Earl Van Dorn." *Southern Historical Society Papers* 19 (January–December 1891): 191–201.

McMinn, W.P. "Service with Van Dorn's Cavalry." *Confederate Veteran* (October 1919): 384–86.

Osborne, Charles M., ed. "The Civil War Letters of Robert W. Banks." *Journal of Mississippi History* 5, no. 3 (July 1943): 141–54.

Parks, George E. "One Story of the 109th Illinois Volunteer Infantry Regiment." *Journal of the Illinois State Historical Society* (Summer 1963): 282–97. Digitized copy located online at dig.lib.niu.edu/ISHS/ishs-1963summer/ishs-1963summer-282.pdf (July 2011).

Parson, Thomas E. "Thwarting Grant's First Drive on Vicksburg: Van Dorn's Holly Springs Raid." *Blue & Gray* 27, no. 3 (2010): 6–26, 42–50.

Politzer, Eric. "Robert Creighton Murphy: U.S. Consul at Shanghai, Brigade Commander, National Scapegoat." *The Association for the Preservation of Historic Congressional Cemetery* newsletter (Fall 2002), 4.

Read, Charles W. "Reminiscences of the Confederate States Navy." *Southern Historical Society Papers* 1 (1876): 331–62.

Roth, Dave. "Earl Van Dorn—More Than Just a Skirt-Chasin' Pretty Boy." *Blue & Gray* 27, no. 3 (2010): 5.

Roth, Dave, and Tom Parson. "The Generals Tour: The Holly Springs Raid." *Blue and Gray* 27, no. 3 (2010): 51–65.

Searcy, M.W. "General Van Dorn's Holly Springs Victory." *Confederate Veteran* 15 (May 1907): 229.

Smith, Brier R. "Major General Mansfield Lovell and the Fall of New Orleans: The Downfall of a Career." Memphis Pink Palace Museum, *Museum Quarterly* 1, no. 3 (Spring 1973).

Stevenson, W.R. "The Capture of Holly Springs, Mississippi." *Confederate Veteran* 9, no. 3 (March 1901): 134.

Still, William. "The Iron Rebel Navy." *Civil War Times Illustrated* 19, no. 3 (June 1980): 22–32.

Stokes, David M. "Railroads Blue and Gray: Rail Transport in the Civil War 1861–1865: A Bibliography." *National Railway Bulletin* 65, no. 5 (2000): 4–11, 32–39.

Williams, Clay. "Last Chance to Save Vicksburg." *Journal of Mississippi History* 60, no. 2 (Spring 1979): 6–19.

Williams, Thomas R. "Documents: Letters of General Thomas Williams, 1862." *American Historical Review* 14 (October 1908–July 1909): 304–28.

Wright, Michael F. "Vicksburg and the Trans-Mississippi Supply Line 1861–1863." *Journal of Mississippi History* 48 (1979): 210–25.

MANUSCRIPTS (LETTERS, DIARIES)

Bagart, R.D. Letter written from USS *Richmond*. July 17, 1862. Mississippi Department of Archives and History, Library Division. Special collections. Manuscript collection.

Chadwell, Alexander H. Diary. Used with permission of Susan Chadwell Dignard and the cooperation of Kenneth Hurt and Bob Schmidt.

"Clint to Hannah." Letter. January 1, 1863. U.S. Grant Presidential Papers. Congressional and Political Research Center. Mississippi State University Library.

Hillyer, Anna. Letter. 1862. Headquarters, 13th Army Corps, Army of the Tennessee, Office of the Provost Marshal General. U.S. Grant Presidential Papers. Congressional and Political Research Center. Mississippi State University Library.

Pomeroy, Fletcher. Diary. Co. D, 7th Kansas Cavalry. Used with permission of his great-grandson Don Paul.

ONLINE

Anon. "The Mississippi Central Railroad Campaign," www.angelfire.com/ms2/grantshilohvicksburg.

Bowen, Benjamin. "The Exploits of Waul's Texas Legion." freepages.family.rootsweb.ancestry.com/~bowen/waulslegion.html.

Bright, David L. "Confederate Railroads." www.csa-railroads.com.

Ezell, Norman L. "The Tragedy at Duck Hill Station: Collision of the *James Brown* and the *A.M. West*." genealogytrails.com/miss/montgomery/trainwreck.html.

Gift, George W. "The Story of the *Arkansas*." www.missouridivision-scv.org/mounits/cssark.htm.

Hills, Parker. "Grant's Vicksburg Supply Line: Myth or Fact?" Civil War Trust. civilwar.org/battlefields/vicksburg/vicksburg-history-articles/vicksburgsupplyhillpg.html.

Hunt, Kathy Kelly. "Biography of John Summerfield Griffith." The Kaufman County TX GenWeb Project Site. www.txgenweb5.org/txkaufman/civilwar/biogriff.htm.

Mickle, John. "Van Dorn Raid." marshallcountyms.org/military/vandorn.php.

Stewart, Tom. "From Whence We Came: A Readable Story of Early Holly Springs." *The South Reporter* (April 15, 2005). www.southreporter.com/2005/wk15/features.html.

Williams, Scott. "Missourians or Volunteers from Missouri Units on the Ironclad *Arkansas*." www.missouridivision-scv.org/mounits/cssark.htm.

NEWSPAPER ARTICLES

Mason, Mrs. Carrington. "Raid on Holly Springs." *Memphis Commercial Appeal*, May 30, 1901.

Missouri Democrat. "Particulars of the Rebel Raid into Holly Springs." January 5, 1863. Author's collection.

Mobile Register and Advertiser, December 27, 1862.

About the Author

D r. Brandon H. Beck is the author of eight books on Civil War history. He is the founder and director of the McCormick Civil War Institute at Shenandoah University in Winchester, Virginia. He currently lives in Columbus, Mississippi, and teaches part time at East Mississippi Community College.

Visit us at

www.historypress.net